POSSESSION

by Sasha Hails

FOR AMATEUR PRODUCTION ENQUIRIES

UNITED KINGDOM AND WORLD
EXCLUDING NORTH AMERICA
licensing@concordtheatricals.co.uk
020-7054-7298

Each title is subject to availability from Concord Theatricals,
depending upon country of performance.

The moral right of Sasha Hails to be identified as author of this work has been asserted in accordance with Section 77 of the Copyright, Designs and Patents Act 1988.

USE OF COPYRIGHTED MUSIC

A licence issued by Concord Theatricals to perform this play does not include permission to use the incidental music specified in this publication. In the United Kingdom: Where the place of performance is already licensed by the PERFORMING RIGHT SOCIETY (PRS) a return of the music used must be made to them. If the place of performance is not so licensed then application should be made to PRS for Music (www.prsformusic.com). A separate and additional licence from PHONOGRAPHIC PERFORMANCE LTD (www.ppluk.com) may be needed whenever commercial recordings are used. Outside the United Kingdom: Please contact the appropriate music licensing authority in your territory for the rights to any incidental music.

USE OF COPYRIGHTED THIRD-PARTY MATERIALS

Licensees are solely responsible for obtaining formal written permission from copyright owners to use copyrighted third-party materials (e.g., artworks, logos) in the performance of this play and are strongly cautioned to do so. If no such permission is obtained by the licensee, then the licensee must use only original materials that the licensee owns and controls. Licensees are solely responsible and liable for clearances of all third-party copyrighted materials, and shall indemnify the copyright owners of the play(s) and their licensing agent, Concord Theatricals Ltd., against any costs, expenses, losses and liabilities arising from the use of such copyrighted third-party materials by licensees.

IMPORTANT BILLING AND CREDIT REQUIREMENTS

If you have obtained performance rights to this title, please refer to your licensing agreement for important billing and credit requirements.

POSSESSION was first produced on Thursday 15 June– Saturday 15 July 2023 at the Arcola Theatre, London. The cast was as follows:

HOPE / MERCY............................ Diany Samba-Bandza
ALICE YOUNG / ALICE SEELEY HARRIS ..... Dorothea Myer-Bennett
KASAMBAYI ....Sarah Amankwah
JOHN DENT / JOHN HARRIS....................... Milo Twomey
DAVID / GEORGES / GEORGES' FATHER / NSALA ..Nedum Okonyia

Content Warning – Child birth, sexual content, discussions of sexual violence against women, discussions of generational trauma, historical photography of amputated body parts.
Age Suitability – 15+

Writer | Sasha Hails
Director | Oscar Pearce
Associate Director | Tramaine Reindorf
Designer | Sarah Beaton
Lighting Designer | Joseph Ed Thomas
Video Designer | Leo Flint
Costume Supervisor | Alexandra Kharibian
Sound Designer | Esther Kehinde Ajayi (EKAS)
Production Manager | Josephine Tremmeling
Production Assistant | Defne Ozdogan
Movement Director | Tian Brown-Sampson
Stage Manager | Alex Jaouen
Lingala coach | Antho Lusambo Atangowena
Puppetry Consultant | Josie Daxter

CHARACTERS

Present Day

HOPE – 19, Black British Congolese girl. Kasambayi's daughter.

KASAMBAYI – 40ish, Black Congolese, first generation immigrant. Hope's Mother.

ALICE YOUNG – 41, White, foreign correspondent.

JOHN DENT – 49ish, White, foreign correspondent.

DAVID, GEORGES' FATHER – 16

DAVID – 22, Hope's lover

GEORGES – 22, Hope's son

BUS DRIVER, PARTY GIRL, YOUNG GYM BOY, MORGUE ASSISTANT, CHAIR, LECTURE HALL ASSISTANT

1900

ALICE SEELEY HARRIS – 30s, English missionary wife.

JOHN HARRIS – 49, English missionary.

NSALA – 22, Congolese man.

MERCY – 13, Congolese girl

AUTHOR'S NOTES

This play has had a long creative journey and I am incredibly grateful for all who have been part of helping it along the way.

It began from a very personal place. I wanted to explore all the challenges, emotional and financial, around being a working mother, and the ongoing frustrations and guilt I felt about being torn between work and home. I decided to make my character Alice a foreign correspondent, one of the toughest jobs for a Mother, that takes you far from home and into danger. As I began researching, interviewing the extraordinary Maggie O'Kane and Victoria Brittain, and reading about Lee Miller, Janine de Giovanni and Martha Gelhorn, I realised that this wasn't such a personal problem, it was common and it was political. This 'guilt' I felt at my ambition for a whole world beyond the family and raising children was not just born from my own emotional connection to my children, it was societal. It was Victoria Brittain who suggested that the Democratic Republic of Congo might be the place to set my play, in the heart of Africa, where the dual horrors of the colonisation and exploitation of women and of the colonisation and exploitation of the earth meet. Just at this time, in a strange coincidence, I signed up to house a refugee and Antho Lusambo Atangowena came to live with us, a Congolese asylum seeker. She shared her compelling life story and her spirit inspired the character of Kasambayi and her daughter Hope. But the play was still missing something.

One day, researching King Leopold's Congo, Alice Seeley Harris appeared on my computer screen, rising up like a ghost with her photographs. The links between the mining of cobalt and coltan today and the rubber trade in King Leopold's Congo were immediately apparent. It is horrific and shocking to see how history continues to repeat itself.

NOTES ON STAGING

Alice Seeley Harris and John Harris are historical characters. The other characters are fictional but inspired by close research. Alice Young and Alice Seeley Harris should be played by the same actor. John Dent and John Harris should be played by the same actor. The actor playing David (Georges' Father) should also play David (Hope's lover in the Congo), Georges (Hope's son), and Nsala. The actor playing Hope should also play Mercy.

ACKNOWLEDGMENTS

Thanks first to my three daughters, Siofra, Grainne and Cara who taught me so much about life and mothering, and who have been seminal part of the creative conversations around *Possession* throughout its development. Thank you to Simon Reade for planting the seed of the play when he commissioned the monologue *My Front Line* and Alison Reid for her performance as Helen, an early version of Alice Young. Thank you to Maggie O'Kane and Victoria Brittain for sharing their stories. Thank you to Anne Edyvean who produced *My Front Line* on the radio and helped develop it further with Fiona Shaw. To Caitlin Mcleod who when I returned to the monologue some years later wanting to expand it into a longer play was brilliant at interrogating it with me. Thanks also to Madani Younis, Stewart Pringle, Deidre O'Halloran and Mark Rosenblatt who helped grow it further.

Thank you to Antho Lusambo Atangowena, who lived with us for two years and who so generously shared her story, her culture and her community with me and who is the inspiration behind Kasambayi. She has waited ten years to be given asylum in England and is still waiting.

Thanks to the readers who gave their precious time and their very thoughtful and insightful advice and helped me interrogate and question the script: Jenny Mcleish, Isabella Tree, Suze Hails, Jackie Christie, Chelsea Bondzanga, David Kimbangyi, Juliet Benis. Also Dominic Dromgoole, Michael Nest, Kevin Fitzmaurice, and Hugh Kinsala Cunningham.

Thanks to my agent, Jennie Miller for her endless support, and thanks to the Arcola, and Leyla and Mehmet for believing in the play and providing it with a home. Thanks also to Rebecca Seeley Harris; Rowena and Quentin Seddon; Charlie Burrell; Mick and Carole Pearce; Patty and Michael Hopkins, and Damian Lewis. And finally thank you to Oscar, my amazing director, for his patience, vision and passion – and the wonderful team of hugely talented cast and creatives he gathered to bring it to life.

CAST

DIANY SAMBA-BANDZA | HOPE/MERCY

Diany's theatre credits include: *Henry V* at the Donmar Warehouse directed by Max Webster; *A Christmas Carol* at The Bridge Theatre directed by Nicholas Hytner & Never Look Back for English Touring Theatre.

Screen credits include: *The Witcher, The Diplomat* (NETFLIX); *Intergalactic* (Sky); *Anansi Boys, Jack Ryan* (Amazon).

DOROTHEA MYER-BENNETT | ALICE YOUNG / ALICE SEELEY HARRIS.

Trained at Bristol Old Vic Theatre School.

Theatre includes: *Leopoldstadt* (Wyndhams) Shaw Shorts; *While The Sun Shines, The Lottery of Love* and *The Philanderer* (Orange Tree); *Holy Sh!t* (Kiln Theatre); *The Winslow Boy* (Chichester Festival Theatre); *Merchant of Venice* (Shakespeare's Globe/Lincoln Centre, New York); *Pericles* (Shakespeare's Globe); *Creditors* and *Miss Julie* (Jermyn Street Theatre); *Rosenbaum's Rescue* (Park Theatre); *Richard III* and *Uncle Vanya* (West Yorkshire Playhouse); *The Misanthrope* (Bristol Old Vic); *Hay Fever* (Royal Exchange Theatre); *She Stoops To Conquer* (Birmingham Repertory Theatre); *Restoration* (Headlong); *Much Ado About Nothing, As You Like It, Arcadia, Two Gentlemen of Verona, Richard III, The Cherry Orchard, King Lear* and *The Comedy of Errors* (Shakespeare at the Tobacco Factory Theatre); *This was a Man* (Finborough Theatre); *The Fitzrovia Radio Hour* (St James Theatre); *The Spire* (Salisbury Playhouse); *Present Laughter* (UK tour); *Mendelssohn* in Scotland (City of London Sinfonia) and *The Tamer Tamed* (Shakespeare's Globe/Sam Wanamaker Festival).

Television includes: *Juice, The Chelsea Detective, Dodger, Doc Martin, Before We Die, Around the World in 80 Days, Holby City, Plastic People* and *Jude the Obscure/Dead Man Talking*.

Film includes: *The Honourable Rebel, The Payback, The Orchard* and *Ladies*.

SARAH AMANKWAH | KASAMBAYI

Sarah trained at Manchester School of Theatre and has worked in a broad range of projects for stage and screen. Most recently she featured in the feature film *Dungeons and Dragons: Honor Among Thieves* as Baroness Torbo.

Theatre includes: *Henry V, Henry IV: Part I & Part II, Richard III, Globe Ensemble, Doctor Faustus, 'Tis Pity She's a Whore* (Shakespeare's Globe); *Amadeus, The Threepenny Opera, Death & The King's*

Horseman (National Theatre); *The Crucible, Skriker* (Manchester Royal Exchange); *The Lion King* (Lyceum Theatre, West End); *De Gabay* (National Theatre of Wales); *Tiata Tamba Tamba* (Tiata Fahodzi); *Shakespeare 365, Spring Shakespeare* (Orange Tree Theatre); *Six Characters in Search of an Author, A Midsummer Night's Dream* (Aquila Theatre, US Tour); *Fair Trade* (Latitude Festival, Rich Mix & Edinburgh Festival); *Rumpelstiltskin & Alice: Through the Looking Glass* (Edinburgh Festival); *24 Hour Plays* (Old Vic Theatre); *Faithful Russian* (Manchester Met).

Television includes: *Doctor Who* (BBC); *Black Earth Rising* (BBC/ Netflix); *Marcella* (ITV/Buccaneer Media); *The Damnation of Darwin* (HBO).

Film includes: *Dungeons & Dragons, World War Z* (Paramount Pictures).

MILO TWOMEY | JOHN DENT / JOHN HARRIS

Recent theatre credits include: *Winter solstice* (Orange Tree); *Mary Poppins* (UK tour); *Twelfth Night* (Sheffield Crucible); *Much Ado About Nothing* (Manchester Royal Exchange); *Richard III* (Nottingham Playhouse); *Dancing At Lughnasa* (Royal & Derngate); *Phoenix of Madrid/Surprise Of Love* (Bath); *I Heart Peterborough/Dandy In The Underworld* (Soho); *Brief Encounter* (Kneehigh UK/US tour); *Lady Widermere's Fan, Blithe Spirit, The Children's Hour, She Stoops To Conquer, Harvey* (Manchester Royal Exchange); *Canterbury Tales* (RSC West End).

Recent TV credits include: *Four Lives, Motherfatherson, Informer, War Of The Worlds, Father Brown, Cuffs, War And Peace* (BBC); *The Thief, His Wife And The Canoe, Marcella, Endeavour* (ITV); *A Discovery Of Witches*, Agatha Raisin (Sky), *Avenue 5* (HBO); *The Feed* (Amazon); *No Offence, Kiri, Man Down* (C4); *Safe, Free Rein* (Netflix); *X Company* (CBC); *Tyrant* (Fox).

Recent film: *Damsel* (Netflix).

NEDUM OKONYIA | DAVID / GEORGES / GEORGES' FATHER / NSALA

Nedum is a British Actor, born in Nigeria. He recently graduated from the Guildford school of Acting with a BA (Hons) in Acting. *Possession* will mark Nedum's professional stage debut. Nedum has a background of stage performing and dance.

CREATIVE TEAM

WRITER | SASHA HAILS

Possession is Sasha's first play. Sasha is currently lead writer and co creator on CBBC's hit fifth series of Enid Blyton's Malory Towers. Recent work includes *Belgravia* (Carnival); *Midwich Cuckoos* (HBO/SKY) and lead writer of Netflix/Nutopia 6 part series *The Last Tsars*, *Versailles* (canal +) and five-part TV adaptation of *The Moonstone* for BBC. Sasha's *Casualty* episode Unsilenced, addressed FGM on Prime Time TV for the first time, was BAFTA nominated and won a BBC Production Award and a Sexual Health Award. Her radio play Best Interests won a MFJ award.

Previous to becoming a writer Sasha was an actress. She acted in Francois Ozon's early films and created numerous devised shows with her company 'Talking Tongues'.

DIRECTOR | OSCAR PEARCE

A highly experienced, award-wining theatre practitioner with over twenty-five years experience in classical, modern and new plays of national and international significance. As an actor he has been in several seasons with the RSC, performed in many of the countries best loved regional theatres, The West End, The Donmar and The Almeida. Internationally he has performed on Broadway, in Paris, Rome, Madrid and Tokyo. He comes from a diverse cultural and politicised background, having been born in Zambia and spent formative years in post independent Zimbabwe moving to London at eighteen to study at The Guildhall School of Music and Drama, he maintains a close relationship with Zimbabwe. This is his 5th engagement with The Arcola, having performed in the acclaimed production of *Jenufa* by Timberlake Wertenbaker and *The Divided Lang* by Patrick Marmion. His directorial debut of Will Self's *Great Apes*, awarded him a nomination for Best Director, in The Stage Debut awards. Other directorial credits include, *Keith?* Arcola Studio 1 and Mike Bartlett's *13* at Jacksons Lane.

ASSOCIATE DIRECTOR | TRAMAINE REINDORF

Tramaine is interested in telling relatable and compelling stories from diverse perspectives. Her directing credits include: *Essentially Black* (Soho Theatre) and *Flat Shoes in the Club?* (Theatre503). As an assistant her credits include: *The Wonderful World of Dissocia* (Theatre Royal Stratford East) and *The Breach* (Hampstead Theatre).

DESIGNER | SARAH BEATON

Sarah is an award-winning performance designer and visual dramaturge. She studied Design for Stage at The Royal Central School of Speech & Drama, graduating in 2011 with First Class Honours. Later that year she was awarded The Linbury Prize for Stage Design.

From 2015–2016 she was the Designer On Attachment at The Old Vic Theatre. Her work has been exhibited at The National Theatre, World Stage Design (Cardiff), the Victoria and Albert Museum and World Stage Design 2017 (Taiwan).

Sarah has designed for venues in the UK and internationally including Sadler's Wells, The Young Vic, Shakespeare's Globe, Manchester Royal Exchange, Trafalgar Studios, Hampstead Theatre, The Oxford Playhouse, Richmond Theatre, The Lowry, Altes Schauspielhaus (Germany), Theatre Rigiblik (Switzerland), Freedom Theatre (Palestine) & Lit Live Festival (India). She is an Associate Artist of Engineer Theatre Collective and a visiting lecturer at the RCSSD.

LIGHTING DESIGNER | JOSEPH ED THOMAS
Training: ArtsEd and RADA.

Joseph has designed shows in London and throughout the UK. West End and Touring Lighting Design Credits: *Dr Zhivago, Annie Get Your Gun, ONCE* (London Palladium); *Collabro, Farewell Tour* (Adelphi Theatre and UK TOUR); *The Secret Garden, CAMELOT* (London Palladium); *John Owen Jones* Tour, *Lucie Jones at Christmas* (Her Majesty's Theatre, St Davids Hall Cardiff); *Collabro*, Greatest Hits Tour (London Palladium and UK TOUR).

Lighting Design Credits: *Under The Black Rock* (Arcola Theatre); *Tango After Dark* (Co-design with Charlie Morgan Jones, Peacock Theatre, Sadler's Wells); *Cabaret Havana, Why the Whales Came* (Mountview); *Little Voice* (UK Tour) as Associate LD for Nic Farman, *The Pleasure Garden* (Above The Stag); *39 and Counting* (PARK Theatre); *Our Girls Our Game* (Alhambra Theatre, Bradford); *Wind in the Willows* (Theatre Royal Norwich, Turbine Theatre and LATITUDE); *EVITA* (Eve Lyons Studio Theatre, PPA); *Well-Behaved Women, John Owen Jones –* Live at Cadogan Hall, *Lucie Jones and David Hunter LIVE!, Collabro, Christmas is Here* (Cadogan Hall); *Rags* (PARK Theatre) as Associate LD for Derek Anderson; *LOST BOYS* (UK TOUR); *A Million Dreams* (O2 Indigo).

VIDEO DESIGNER | LEO FLINT
Leo Flint is a Video Designer, Animator and Creative Director of Studio Flint: a studio specialising in fully integrated, immersive and narrative driven video design for live performance.

Past Design work includes: *PULP* (UK Tour); *Strictly Come Dancing: The Professionals* (UK Tour); *The Making of A Monster* (Wales Millennium Centre); *Lewis Capaldi* (O2 Residency); *Coldplay – Music Of The Spheres* (World Tour); *Richard III* (Royal Shakespeare Company);

David Walliams' Grandpa's Great Escape (UK Tour); *Symphonic Dances* (Royal Opera House); *The Tempest* (Royal Shakespeare Company, The Barbican); *Coldplay – A Head Full of Dreams* (World Tour); *The Curious Incident Of The Dog In The Night-time* (Apollo Theatre London); *Gypsy* (Chichester Festival Theatre and Savoy Theatre, London); *The Light Princess* (National Theatre).

COSTUME SUPERVISOR | ALEXANDRA KHARIBIAN
Alexandra began her career with the National Youth Theatre of Great Britain, touring to the Edinburgh Festival and Paris in 1998. She went on to train at Central Saint Martin's College of Art and Design, graduating with a BA in Design for Performance and London College of Fashion, completing an MA in Costume Design for Performance.

Alexandra has worked in various roles in costume and wardrobe departments as well as a costume supervisor across Theatre, Opera and live events, including Shakespeare's Globe Theatre, The Barbican Theatre, The Royal Opera House, English National Opera, The National Theatre, The Almeida, The Bush Theatre and London 2012 Olympic Ceremonies.

Site-specific live events include Styling for 'The 13th Hour' for Ray Ban, Costume Supervisor for *Grimms Tales* at Shoreditch Town Hall and Stylist for 'Two Sides' Cornetto Unilever Campaign by A Taste of Space. Alexandra is also a visiting Lecturer in Costume at The Guildhall School of Music & Drama.

SOUND DESIGNER | ESTHER KEHINDE AJAYI (EKAS)
A West London-based sound artist. Esther enjoys exploring the nuances of the human condition, particularly the internal politics of self-revelation and authenticity. After returning from Berlin, where she created and completed her two-season-long audio comic, *Dana Is Her Name*, Esther has returned to her London home where she is currently serving London theatre scene sonically alongside studying Sound Arts at the University of Arts London and is excited to begin incorporating technology, theatrical performance and spatial design into her practice. Esther attributes much of her inspiration to the West London sound of the broken beat, the rhythms and harmonies of her Nigerian heritage, and the raw grittiness of London Grime. Esther was an associate artist at theatre company Tiata Fahodzi from 2022–2023 and is excited to continue contributing to British art culture through sonic tone, texture, Sound effects, melody, performance and words.

Sound Design Credits include: *The Dry House* (Marylebone Theatre); *My Brother's Keeper* (Relentless Productions) Theatre 503; *Cash Money* (The Big House); *Talking About A Revolution* (Tiata Fahodzi theatre company); *Hot in here* (Pigfoot Theatre Company); *Yellowman* (Orange Tree Theatre); *Would You Bet Against Us* (Told by An Idiot); *When The Long Trick's Over, All of the conversations/Another fucking play about Race* (ArtsEd); *Athena* (The Yard); *STATEMENTS AFTER AN ARREST UNDER THE IMMORALITY* (Orange Tree Theatre); *Alice* (Landor_ Space, Devised by Three Tree Theatre); *Invisible Light* (Tristan Bates Theatre); *Sad Girls* (Edinburgh Fringe); *Dana is her name* (audio comic).

PRODUCTION MANAGER | JOSEPHINE TREMMELING
Josephine is a production manager, lighting designer and theatre maker. Josephine studied at Dartington College of Arts obtaining a BA Hons in Contemporary Theatre before working as a drama facilitator and co-founding inclusive theatre company Anyone Everyone and Cabaret Troupes The Thrill Billies and The Salacious Sirens. Josephine took the role of technician and later of Production Manager at the Pleasance Theatre for a few glorious years before going freelance both as a PM and Lighting Designer.

Her current projects include National and international tours with Ephemeral Ensemble, Theatre Re, Tangled Feet and The Little Angel Theatre. Recent PM projects include *We Started to Sing* (Arcola); *Hamlet* (National Theatre) and *STARS* (Tamasha Theatre).

PRODUCTION ASSISTANT | DEFNE OZDOGAN
Defne, originally from Istanbul, is a London-based freelance spatial designer currently focused in theatre and performance art. Having completed a BA Architecture course in Central Saint Martins College of Art, she practices stage and production design showcasing works in different scales and narratives. Her artistic approach is inspired by traditional crafts combined with innovative and conscious solutions. She has worked with numerous set designers on commercial and editorial shoots for brands including *Google, La Mer, Numero Magazine, Estee Lauder* and the *Sunday Times.*

MOVEMENT DIRECTOR | TIAN BROWN-SAMPSON
Tian is a director, movement director and producer. Her work centres mainly with Black, East and South East Asian (BESEA) and South Asian theatre work, new writing and promoting diversity, representation and accessibility on-and-off stage and in positions of power and leadership.

Associate/ Movement Directing credits include: *Til Death Do Us Part* (Theatre503); *Two Billion Beats* (Orange Tree Theatre); *Heard* (Camden People's Theatre); and *Spring Awakening the Musical* (SOAS).

Directing credits include: *Two Billion Beats* (Orange Tree Theatre); *In the Black Fantastic* (Southbank Centre); Days of Significance (Arts Ed); *For Her* 还装什么男子汉 (Chinese Arts Now Festival); *Different Book Covers* (Tamasha); *Lost Laowais* (VAULT Festival).

Associate/ Assistant Directing credits include: *Further Than the Furthest Thing* (Young Vic); *A Dead Body in Taos* (Bristol Old Vic, Theatre Royal Plymouth, Wilton's Music Hall, Warwick Arts Centre); *Moreno* (Theatre503); *Gin Craze!* (Royal and Derngate, Northampton); *Does My Bomb Look Big in This?* (Soho Theatre, Tara Arts); and *Forgotten* 遗忘 (Arcola Theatre).

STAGE MANAGER | ALEX JAOUEN

Alex is a graduate from the Royal Central School of Speech and Drama. He has worked as Stage Manager on Book at King's Head Theatre, Theatre503, Seven Dials Playhouse and the Tramshed Theatre. As an Assistant Stage Manager, he has been part of teams at the Kiln Theatre, Donmar Warehouse, Opera Holland Park and the Park Theatre. As a native Hong Konger, Alex is deeply passionate about representing the BESEA community in theatres across London.

arcola
theatre

Arcola Theatre produces daring, high-quality theatre in the heart of East London and beyond.
We commission and premiere exciting, original works alongside rare gems of world drama and bold new productions of classics. Our socially engaged, international programme champions diversity, challenges the status quo, and attracts over 65,000 people to our building each year. Ticket prices are some of the most affordable in London.

Every year, we offer 26 weeks of free rehearsal space to culturally diverse and refugee artists; our Grimeborn Festival opens up opera with contemporary stagings at affordable prices; and our Participation department creates thousands of creative opportunities for the people of Hackney and beyond. Our pioneering environmental initiatives are award-winning and aim to make Arcola the world's first carbon-neutral theatre.

Arcola has won awards including the UK Theatre Award for Promotion of Diversity, The Stage Award for Sustainability and the Peter Brook Empty Space Award.

MEHMET ERGEN
Artistic Director
LEYLA NAZLI
Executive Producer
MILLIE WHITTAM
Marketing Manager
STEVE HAYGREEN
Finance Manager
CHARLOTTE CROFT

Morel

It is not enough to denounce a wrong ; it is necessary to show how that wrong originates, and to put forward a practical remedy.

Blake

O Rose thou art sick.
The invisible worm,
That flies in the night
In the howling storm:

Has found out thy bed
of crimson joy:
And his dark secret love
Does thy heart destroy.

King Leopold's Lament

The Kodak has been a sore calamity to us. The most powerful enemy that has confronted us... The only witness I have encountered in my long career that I couldn't bribe.

ACT ONE

Scene One – London. Twenty-Two Years Ago –

(Silence. A wind. **HOPE** *[nineteen, fierce, whip smart, charismatic, funny] emerges centre stage. We aren't sure how she got there. She has a sense of purpose about her. Something of the ringmaster. Something of the MC. She might smile round at us all. She clicks her fingers – skin on skin –)*

*(***HOPE** *conjures up London Street sounds – and a low, compelling, beckoning drum beat. She sways to the music, letting it into her –)*

(And now she concentrates extra hard. Clicks again – and conjures:)

*(***KASAMBAYI** *[forty five-ish passionate, quietly intelligent, courageous], drags herself onto the stage. She's tired – and heavily pregnant. She lugs all her belongings with her in plastic bags and a broken wheelie suitcase. She wears a mix of Western clothes with African cloth wrapped over.)*

*(***HOPE** *watches* **KASAMBAYI** *intently, critical but with great love. Seeking to understand.)*

(**KASAMBAYI** *drags her bags to a seat. She pulls them up around her. We see she is struggling because she only has one hand.*)

HOPE. *London. The 38 bus. Twenty years ago!*

So now we know where we are.

(**KASAMBAYI** *takes her African cloth and WRAPS it around her head – like a bandage – round and round – blocking out the light – then she gathers her bags around her – and leans her head – wrapped like a chrysalis – and she's asleep –*)

(*The bus pulls up – pings.*)

(*Another couple of late night stragglers get on the bus.* **PARTY GIRL** *and a young bloke in gym stuff.*)

(**KASAMBAYI** *gives a huge moan. She still has the cloth wrapped around her head.*)

DRIVER. Victoria Station. Victoria Station. This bus has terminated. Everyone off please.

(**KASAMBAYI** *leans on the seat in front of her in full labour. Moaning. In agony. The* **DRIVER** *comes to persuade her off –*)

I'm sorry Madam. Off the bus now please.

KASAMBAYI. Je ne peux pas. I can't move. Aaahhhhggghh.

DRIVER. Everyone off. We're terminating here.

PARTY GIRL. For fuck's sake. She's having a baby.

DRIVER. She can't have a baby on my bus.

(*Suddenly with a huge moan* **KASAMBAYI**'s *waters break… her contractions hit hard. She is in full labour immediately –*)

Jesus. It's the fucking Niagara Falls.

PARTY GIRL. Call an ambulance – just call an ambulance – now!

> *(It's all chaos – young gym bloke gets on his phone, **PARTY GIRL**, **HOPE** and the **DRIVER** gather round **KASAMBAYI** trying to help. **HOPE** unwraps **KASAMBAYI**'s head – **KASAMBAYI** emerges from the Chrysalis.)*

Where are you from love? – Do you have anyone we can call? –

KASAMBAYI. Nobody. No one. This baby coming that's all I've got. *(She keeps repeating this and similar...)*

> *(She gives another huge moan –)*

It's coming. I feel it – it's coming – oh Mon Dieu – Notre Père, qui es aux cieux, que ton nom soit sanctifie, que ton regne vienne, que ta volonte soit faite sur la terre comme au ciel... etc...

DRIVER. Jesus –

> *(**PARTY GIRL** dives in to help. She pulls a wet swimming towel out of her bag – and a roll of toilet paper. Gym boy calls an ambulance. Over the following **KASAMBAYI** gives birth – assisted by the **BUS DRIVER** the **PARTY GIRL** and **HOPE**. They deliver the baby using a bottle of Evian – lots of wet wipes – anything they can find.)*

KASAMBAYI. *Donne-nous aujourd'hui notre pain de ce jour. Pardonne-nous nos offences Comme nous pardonnons aussi à ceux qui nous ont offensés. Et ne nous soumets pas à la tentation, mais délivre-nous du mal, car c'est à toi qu'appartiennent le règne, la puissance et la gloire, aux siècles des siècles.*

(*With a huge push the baby is delivered by* **HOPE,** *the* **PARTY GIRL** *and the* **DRIVER** *on the bus seat –* **KASAMBAYI** *holds out her arms with the African cloth –* **HOPE** *places the baby into it – and* **KASAMBAYI** *wraps her and sits exhausted – the cord is still attached – a siren – the paramedics are arriving...*)

(**PARTY GIRL** *and the* **BUS DRIVER** *give each other a hug –* **HOPE** *just stares at* **KASAMBAYI** *and the baby –*)

PARTY GIRL. She's so beautiful – well done – there you go – you're OK now –

KASAMBAYI. Hope.

PARTY GIRL. What's that?

KASAMBAYI. (*Staring into the eyes of new baby.*) Hope.

(**HOPE** *takes the baby from* **KASAMBAYI.**)

HOPE. Hope Victoria Kasambayi Mabele. This is me!

(**HOPE** *rocks her baby self.*)

My name is my story – in four words. It's exactly who I am. I'll show you. We'll start at the end – which is actually my beginning. And roots me.

Mabele is my Congolese family name. I was conceived in Congo, DCR and my Dad was called Fimi Mabele. He came from a small village out in East Congo near Goma.

He had a farm near the mines. I never met him. He was killed by soldiers. Who wanted our crops to feed themselves. Mum said he died saving her life.

He couldn't save her hand though. They cut that off.

Kasambayi is my Mum's name. It was my Granny's name too. All us women in the family share it. It means 'consolation'. Which daughters are – even though they're a disappointment at first because they're not sons. If I'd had a girl I would have called her Kasambayi too.

Victoria is my middle name. Because I was born at Victoria. What my Mum didn't know then was that Victoria wasn't just a station – She was a Queen – of England. Queen of the Industrial Revolution – Queen of colonisation – and her cousin was the devil, King Leopold of Belgium – who claimed the Congo for his own! But hey – it's a powerful British name to put alongside my Congolese names – and I'm a British – Congolese girl.

Hope is my first name. Because that's what I brought into the world with me and that's what my Mum wanted for me. And what I am.

> (**HOPE** *passes her baby self back to* **KASAMBAYI**, *her mother.* **KASAMBAYI** *is helped off the bus and the stage by the* **DRIVER** *and* **PARTY GIRL**.*)*

I lived up to my name for a long time. For sixteen years I was basically a good girl. But round about GCSEs this wind whipped up inside my body and it wouldn't let me be. Like a fire. Like a dance I needed to dance.

At the same time I was going through a really bad patch with Mum. It was like I was allergic to her. I couldn't do her pain anymore. I didn't want to wear her sadness.

Scene Two – London. Hackney. Council Flat. 27th Floor –

(**KASAMBAYI** *sits on the sofa and indicates the seat next to her –*)

KASAMBAYI. Yaka nazalaki kozela yo. *(Come. I'm waiting for you.)* Sit! I've got popcorn. What do you want to watch. Rosie leant me some of her daughter's DVD'S. *The Lion King, Matilda, Anastasia*?

HOPE. Rosie's daughter is six mum. I'm sixteen!

KASAMBAYI. These are classic movies. For everyone.

(**HOPE** *is circling the room. Like a caged animal. She can't sit.*)

We could watch a service with the new pastor on my phone?

(**HOPE** *goes to the little window and puts her face to it, breathes in deeply – sucking in the air –*)

What are you doing over by that window?

HOPE. Oxygenating. I can't breathe. It's summer. Why have you got the heating on?

KASAMBAYI. What's got into you today. Come and sit...

HOPE. Maya's asked me round to her house Mum. To do our homework.

KASAMBAYI. You've been at school all day and hard at work all week. Come sit with me. Take a break.

HOPE. I need to revise. I've got exams soon.

KASAMBAYI. Why don't you call her.

(**HOPE** *hesitates, shakes her head.*)

You see your friends all week. This is time for us!

HOPE. We have SO much time for us. I want to go out.

KASAMBAYI. We can go out. We can go to church.

HOPE. Work, church. Work, church. I know it's enough for you Mum. But it's not enough for me.

KASAMBAYI. When you have had the life/ I've had

HOPE. I know! I know you've had a really hard life. I know about your 'Hard Times'. But It's your Hard Times Mum, not mine.

KASAMBAYI. You don't know anything.

HOPE. And who's fault is that. You won't ever tell me –

KASAMBAYI. What kind of Mother would I be to force such stories on you.

HOPE. But you ARE forcing them on me. Without even telling them. You're so angry.

KASAMBAYI. No I'm not.

HOPE. You are. I feel your pain. Everyone can. I'd rather you talked about it. I want you to.

KASAMBAYI. You don't know what you are asking for.

HOPE. Exactly! That's the problem isn't it! But I want to know! I'm asking...

(**KASAMBAYI** *is about to rage, but instead with a huge strength of will, turns it inwards – turns away from* **HOPE**.)

You're angry now. I can feel it. I wish you'd shout at me! Shout if you want. Tell me off.

(*But* **KASAMBAYI** *has shut off. Gone into her carapace.*)

(**HOPE** *stares at her frustrated.*)

I'm going out then.

KASAMBAYI. Take the popcorn. I won't eat it. Nazwi yango mpo na yo. *(I got it for you.)*

> *(**HOPE** turns back to us, giving up on her mother.)*

HOPE. I wish she had trusted me with the truth – 'cos then I wouldn't have needed to go hunting for it myself.

> *(But **HOPE** is irrepressible. Nothing can hold her down for long...)*

HOPE. I needed life. The sky. The green trees. Nature.

> *(She conjures and the stage floods with green light – it becomes a park. Birdsong. A young black boy, **DAVID** (sixteen), saunters/dances into the middle of it – every fibre of him alive and strong and singing –)*

That was the best summer. The summer of being sixteen.

Scene Three – A Cemetery Park, Hackney
– A Few Years Before–

HOPE. Out in the park it was all velvet sky and hot recycled city breath. Our Savannah –

DAVID. There was a paddling pool and we would wade in.

HOPE. Mothers and toddlers would leave as we arrived.

DAVID. Scatter.

HOPE. We scattered them.

DAVID. Our pack.

HOPE. We were powerful and strong and this was our moment and our watering hole.

DAVID. We rolled kisses between us like dragons roll fire. That summer was ours.

> (*Sound effects. Sunday church bells peel out post service...and continue peeling into the next scene as –*)

> (**HOPE** *looks across the stage, to see...*)

Scene Four – The Same Cemetery Park, Hackney 1900's –

(**ALICE SEELEY HARRIS** [*Thirties, missionaries wife, dutiful, intrepid, capable, compassionate, loyal*] *pushes a huge old-fashioned Silver Cross Edwardian pram through an English park and takes a seat on a bench. She is heavily pregnant.*)

(*Across the park comes hurrying towards her a vicar –* **JOHN HARRIS** [*Forties, missionary. Old school British Colonial Patriarch. Ambitious, religious, zealous.*] *He is carrying a box.*)

(*They beam at each other – clearly in love –*)

(**JOHN** *holds out an unwieldy box, beautifully wrapped.*)

JOHN. For you!

ALICE. John! Thank you.

(*She takes it and weighs it in her hands. It's heavy –*)

(*Playful.*) Something for baby?

(**JOHN** *puts his hand on the gift, stopping her –*)

JOHN. Wait. Perhaps I have done this the wrong way round – I have news first –

(**JOHN** *takes* **ALICE**'s *hands. Sits her down gently, serious.*)

HOPE. I found these two in my cemetery park – still hanging out – or maybe they found me – unfinished business – they may have been gone over a hundred years but they're still not done –

JOHN. It's the news we've been hoping for.

ALICE. *(Her face lights up.)* We can have the lease on the cottage?

> *(Tiny beat.)*

JOHN. A different sort of news. It's not really about home – well it is – but –

ALICE. You got the placement?

JOHN. Yes.

> *(**ALICE** claps her hands. Delighted.)*

ALICE. Where?

JOHN. The Congo Free State

> *(**ALICE** looks confused –)*

Africa! King Leopold of Belgium's colony.

ALICE. King Leopold?

JOHN. The papers call him a "philanthropic monarch!" He's helping the Congolese farm rubber – helping them enter the biggest new market in the West – rubber tyres for automobiles – he is working with Dunlop – And he's welcoming Christian missionaries with open arms.

> *(**ALICE** holds **JOHN**'s hands, her eyes lighting in excitement.)*

ALICE. When do they want us?

JOHN. Soon. As soon as we can after the baby comes – how long will you need?

ALICE. I don't know – a good few weeks – I'll need to recover from the birth and they'll be such a lot to organise – How long will we be there?

JOHN. Two years at least – possibly four –

ALICE. Four years! *(Thinking fast and furious, excited.)* I'll have to get shoes for the children to grow into – fabrics, muslins, linens – will we take a nurse with us John – I will need some help?

> *(Beat.* **JOHN** *looks at* **ALICE**. *Something she hasn't understood.)*

JOHN. We can't take the children Alice.

> *(Beat.* **ALICE** *stares. Floored.)*

I thought you knew that –

> *(Beat –)*

ALICE. I can't go without the children.

JOHN. It wouldn't be safe. The heat. The tropical diseases. The wild animals. And we have work to do. I need you to help me –

ALICE. I know that but –

JOHN. There's a school for The children of Missionaries – Harley House.

ALICE. I'd like them with us John. I think they'd be better off with us –

JOHN. It will take a good few weeks by boat – then miles into the centre of Africa – We're heading into the unknown. It would be reckless indeed to take them. Foolhardy, and selfish.

ALICE. But four years?

JOHN. God will guide us.

ALICE. Four years! That is a lifetime for a small child. And what if we fell ill – what if – what if we were never to return?

> (**JOHN** *stares at* **ALICE** – *fighting intense disappointment* –)

JOHN. My whole life up to this point has been leading to this –

> (**ALICE** *takes* **JOHN***'s hand. She puts it on her tight swollen abdomen* –)

ALICE. And this John. And this –

> (**JOHN***'s face changes momentarily as he feels the baby move – he is torn. He searches* **ALICE***'s face.*)

JOHN. You knew what it meant to be a missionary wife.

ALICE. I did. I do. But –

JOHN. I love our children too. I will miss them too. But a congregation of souls out there have already invested their faith in us. They are waiting.

ALICE. I don't know if I can –

> (**JOHN** *has an idea for a new approach* –)

JOHN. What can you remember of your early childhood?

ALICE. Riding on my Father's shoulders. Mother telling me off for eating blackberries – my little sister in a cradle by the fire – not much.

> (**ALICE** *shakes her head as the memories fade* –)

JOHN. A handful of memories. That is all any of us have of our early years. So maybe it doesn't matter how they are spent as long as we are warm, well fed and surrounded by kindness –

> (*Tiny beat.* **ALICE** *isn't totally convinced* –)

ALICE. What do you remember?

JOHN. The smell of leather. Being taught to polish my boots. Wax on the bristles –

ALICE. What do you remember of your mother?

> (**JOHN** *shakes his head. Nothing.*)

Do you wish you could have known her better?

> (**JOHN** *stiffens.*)

JOHN. I didn't lack for love. I got love from God – from teachers at my boarding school – from friends – you have to learn to trust the world – I learned independence – it stood me in good stead. I don't think I've done badly for myself?

ALICE. Maybe it gave you that determination and edge that makes you so singular – but you had to put your heart on one side and concentrate on your mind – it's not the only way.

> (**JOHN** *takes* **ALICE**'s *hand again – listening to her kindness he knows he needs her more than ever.*)

JOHN. Family can be a trap. We have a duty to our children of course – but as a preacher I must also think of the other souls entrusted to my care.

ALICE. Couldn't we wait until they are a little older – a child needs to know where it belongs John – who it belongs to –

JOHN. You are confusing belonging and love Alice. Our children don't belong to us. They belong to the world. To God.

ALICE. I know my duty and service lie at your side but –

JOHN. It is not only me who asks for your duty and service Alice. It is God.

ALICE. I am afraid.

(**JOHN** *puts his hands on hers. Passionate, gentle, persuasive.*)

JOHN. I am afraid too. It is frightening to serve something greater than ourselves. To serve God's Will we must surrender our own. But He does not demand that our Wills be crushed. Only that we become pliant to Him as the willow twig is to the practiced hand. That we embrace suffering as a way towards an understanding of love –

(*A beat –* **ALICE** *looks unconvinced –* **HOPE** *still watching – comments cheekily –*)

HOPE. Takes all sorts of God to make a world –

(*To* **ALICE**.)

That's his version – you don't have to agree –

(*Does* **ALICE** *hear* **HOPE**? *We don't know. She is struggling...*)

JOHN. Remember – Isaiah, chapter 6, verse 8,

"Also I heard the voice of the Lord saying, Whom shall I send and who will go for us?" What was the answer? What?

ALICE. (*Sotto, riposte.*) Here I am; Send me.

(*Over the next* **JOHN** *holds* **ALICE**'s *hand tight – pouring his enthusiasm into her –*)

JOHN. We knew we could be sent to the wildest regions – Remember Isaiah – what was the answer?

ALICE. Here I am; Send me.

JOHN. We are going to open to civilisation, the only part of our globe which it has not yet penetrated. We are going to pierce the darkness which hangs over entire peoples. Remember Isaiah.

ALICE. *(Finding strength in* **JOHN***'s eyes.)* Here I am; Send me.

JOHN. Have we not pledged our lives to work for the solemn and awful charge of spiritual formation...?

ALICE. *(Crying now.)* I will miss them so much John.

JOHN. *(Holding her.)* Of course you will.

> (**HOPE** *sits beside* **ALICE**. *Puts a hand on her to comfort her. Listens with her.)*

(Gentle, paternal.) Sometimes, in our disappointment over what we don't have, or can't have – we fail to appreciate the significance of what God has given us.

God has given you children Alice. He has also given you the opportunity to spread his word. It seems to me he has given you all –

> (**ALICE** *nods, holding back her tears. Brave. The toddler in the pram stirs, cries, she rocks the pram –)*

> (**JOHN** *hands her the wrapped gift again. She dries her tears. Puts on a smile. Opens it –)*

> *(To reveal a Kodak camera.)*

ALICE. What is it?

JOHN. A camera. You can take pictures of the children for us to take with us – and you can document and record our time in the Congo and send the pictures back to the children. So they can keep abreast of all we are doing – so they can share in our endeavour.

ALICE. Thank you. Thank you.

> (**JOHN** *takes the camera –)*

JOHN. Here. Let me take one of you now.

(**ALICE** *smiles – puts a hand on her belly – the other rocking the pram – she stares into the camera.*)

(**HOPE** *photobombs them – making a V sign – smiling into the camera too –* **JOHN** *and* **ALICE** *remain unaware –*)

(*As* **JOHN** *and* **ALICE** *move away we are left with* **HOPE**.)

Scene Five – The Same Cemetery Park, Hackney – A Few Years Ago –

(**HOPE** *and* **DAVID** *reprise their moment from scene four –*)

HOPE. Out here in this cemetery park is where it happened.

(*She throws down a picnic blanket – she sits on it under the following and* **DAVID** *joins her.*)

DAVID. You took your time.

HOPE. I got held up.

DAVID. Thought you'd changed your mind.

HOPE. Got my exams you know.

DAVID. Girl like you don't need to study –

HOPE. Yeah?

DAVID. Yeah.

HOPE. Boy like you do.

DAVID. Nah, I'm going to the university of life!

HOPE. Nice. What they teach you there?

DAVID. Everything you can't learn from books.

HOPE. What's that then?

(*The tension fizzes between them. It's clear what's going to happen.*)

And I was only sixteen but I wanted someone inside me. I needed someone inside me. I liked the way my body knew more than I did. Knew how to respond. And I loved the way my mind followed. A hand that stroked and searched set off a trail of stars that melted my brain and ran back like a river down inside me.

My body had a mind of it's own and it just wanted to open and let the world in! So I did.

And soon I realised I'd let more than the world in.

> (**HOPE** *takes out her phone. She takes a few selfies, focussing on her big belly – enjoying her pregnant silhouette.*)
>
> (*Suddenly – with a loud bang her tummy bursts!*)

I'd let in a baby. I was pregnant with Georges.

> (*She gasps in shock and horror –*)
>
> (*Other bangs follow – bullets – guns – screams and shouts.*)
>
> (**HOPE** *panics – runs – tries to escape but is caught up in the changing set – she dodges and weaves – and finally finds her way off into the wings.*)

Scene Six – A Hotel Room. Lubumbashi, Congo Present Day –

(Yelling and shouting and loud music pumping. A protest is taking place outside.)

(Suddenly the crack of a gun. Screams and shouts. Something has disrupted the crowd.)

*(***ALICE YOUNG*** stumbles in [forty-ish, foreign correspondent] She is dishevelled. Blood runs down her face behind her ear.)*

(It's a simple hotel room – Modern. Anodyne. Basic. TV and WiFi and all the mod cons. The only clue to where we are is a nod to African heritage with the patterns on the pillows and furnishings. Women's' clothes scattered on the Heart of Darkness *by Joseph Conrad lies on the bed and* Colbalt Red *by Sidhart Kara, and* Coltan *by 'Nest'. A simple holdall on a desk in the corner.)*

*(***ALICE*** grabs a towel. puts it to her head to staunch the bleeding. Pain. Fear. Shock. She fights it.)*

*(***JOHN DENT*** [fifty-ish, white, foreign correspondent, longer in the tooth than Alice, a few more war wounds, but still hungry] staggers in close behind, lugging his broadcast camera and equipment. He dumps it on the floor. Hurries to ***ALICE****.)*

JOHN. Let me see.

(He examines the wound, tender, firm. Capable, competent.)

Fucking hell that was a close shave.

*(He starts to clean the wound with sterilised wet wipes from his camera bag. **ALICE** fights to stop herself trembling.)*

ALICE. What happened to the woman beside me?

JOHN. Let me staunch the bleed.

ALICE. The one carrying the little boy.

JOHN. She's OK.

(Something in his voice.)

ALICE. She fell?

*(**JOHN** doesn't answer.)*

I saw her fall?

JOHN. She was OK.

ALICE. How about her little boy? I waved at him. He waved back.

*(**JOHN** doesn't say anything. Tends the wound.)*

What happened?

*(Beat. **ALICE** pushes **JOHN**'s hand down from her wound.)*

*(She meets **JOHN**'s eyes. Reads the truth.)*

JOHN. It was an accident. It could have been you. Could have been me.

ALICE. *(Disbelief.)* They shot him?

JOHN. It was immediate. He wouldn't have felt anything.

ALICE. Did you get it?

> *(His face and hesitation tells us – yes he did get the shot of the dead child.)*

For fucks sake.

> *(**ALICE** forces her upset into action mode. Channels grief into adrenalin. She picks up John's camera, pushes it at him and goes to the window.)*

Come on.

JOHN. Tidy yourself up first?

ALICE. No. Let them see it how it is.

> *(**JOHN** hesitates. This isn't the way it's done.)*

> *(**ALICE** goes over to the window. Pulls back the blind. Pulls open the curtain. Stands in front of it. Outside the noise of the crowd is dispersing.)*

Ready.

> *(**JOHN** reluctantly raises his camera.)*

JOHN. Too much back light.

ALICE. Just shoot.

> *(**JOHN** decides not to argue, moves round a bit.)*

JOHN. OK. Running.

> *(**ALICE** switches into professional mode. She's good.)*

ALICE. This is Alice Young, reporting from Kolwezi, in the Democratic Republic of Congo. Outside what began as a demonstration by artisanal Cobalt miners against the conditions at the mines, has transformed into a full scale riot.

In an attempt to control the growing crowd the Army were sent in. Trucks were set on fire and a battalion of fully armed FARDC soldiers swarmed the area and suppressed the mob with gunfire. Numerous homes and businesses are burning. Civilians caught in the cross fire are unfortunately among those killed.

(**ALICE** *indicates her wound still bleeding.*)

The same bullet which skinned my temple here, lodged itself fatally in a toddler, about three yards to the left of me. His mother was running with him to find safety. He bled to death in her arms.

(**ALICE** *falls silent a moment.*)

(**JOHN** *hesitates. Has she finished? But this was the prelude. She gathers herself and launches in –*)

Cobalt – the Congo's latest miracle mineral is at the bottom of this violence.

Cobalt is an essential component to every lithium-ion rechargeable battery made today, the batteries that power our smartphones, tablets, laptops, and electric vehicles. Roughly seventy five percent of the world's supply of cobalt is mined in the Congo, here where I am today, often by women and children in sub-human conditions.

But it's mega-tech corporations, Apple, Tesla, Google – who are benefitting by turning a blind eye to the horrors and corruption and confusion. The bully only survives because he is unchallenged by the bystander. It suits the West to play ignorant. To keep the Congo in chaos. Because under the cover of this chaos, the most intricately run web of global tech corporations are thriving.

(**JOHN** *puts down his camera.*)

What?

(**JOHN** *sits on the bed.*)

JOHN. We can't use that. You know we can't.

ALICE. I haven't finished. Come on.

(**JOHN** *shakes his head.*)

What's the point if we're not going to tell it like it is.

JOHN. We've got some good footage from the streets we can use.

ALICE. One dead Congolese toddler isn't enough of a story? Is that it?

JOHN. Alice.

ALICE. Maybe I should have been killed. You would get a story out of that – front page – a feature – In the trojan horse of the death of – god forbid – one white foreign correspondent!

JOHN. Alice.

(*Suddenly Alice's phone rings. She snatches it up. Her whole demeanour changing as she does.*)

(**HOPE** *walks into the scene. Leans against the wall – observing quietly –*)

ALICE. Hi Hope – yes – sure – of course – put him on. Louis? Hello darling. Mama loves you. Here. Here's a kiss for you to catch. Here. (**ALICE** *kisses the palm of her hand loudly, cradles it as if it has weight, blows it off loudly.*) Love you Louis. Bye bye!

(*She hangs up.* **HOPE** *remains watching.* **ALICE** *turns back to* **JOHN**.)

He likes to catch kisses. He keeps them in his pocket. He says they all have a different weight. He says his pockets are full of kisses.

JOHN. How old is he now?

ALICE. Two. And a half.

JOHN. Who's Hope?

ALICE. His nanny – childminder – other mother!

>   (**HOPE** *smiles – likes being talked about –)*

>   (**JOHN** *segue-ways, careful but curious.)*

JOHN. I'm sorry it didn't work out with Guy.

ALICE. It was a mis match. We only gave it a go because I was pregnant.

>   *(Beat. Uneasy – some unspoken past here –)*

How are your kids?

JOHN. Good Thanks. Grown up. Tara is twenty one. At Bristol reading philosophy. Nicolas is in his last year at school. And the twins have just done their GCSEs.

ALICE. Wow.

JOHN. I know.

>   *(Beat.)*

ALICE. And your wife?

JOHN. The same.

>   *(A beat.)*

I've missed you.

>   (**ALICE** *looks to him but doesn't answer.)*

>   *(Suddenly her phone rings again. Her face lights up. She answers.)*

ALICE. Louis! Yes darling! I'm coming home very soon. I can't come tonight because I'm working. What was that sweetheart? Chicks?

> (**ALICE** *puts the phone on loudspeaker so* **JOHN** *can hear Louis' voice. She beams.*)

LOUIS. *(Voice over.)* The eggs happened. They were were borned out. One, two, five, four, seven, all of them.

> (**JOHN** *can't help smiling too. The joy and excitement in Louis' voice is tangible.*)

ALICE. *(Into phone.)* Oh My God that's wonderful! That's so exciting! Louis??? *(To* **JOHN**, *clicking off loudspeaker.)* He's run off. That's what he does on the phone, tells a story and then disappears. *(She turns back to the phone.)* Hope? That's so cool. Brilliant. OK. Sure. Yes. You go! Bye!!!

JOHN. Do you live in the country?

ALICE. No. Still the flat in Clapton. No. They're here.

JOHN. Here????

ALICE. Yeah. In the suburbs of Kinshasa.

JOHN. You're joking?

> (**ALICE** *smiles, amused at* **JOHN***'s shock.*)

ALICE. Just for a few months. A farm. We're housesitting.

JOHN. You've brought your kid out here?

ALICE. Relax. I'm renting an old colonial paradise. Walls and gates and security guards. Their housekeeper and cook are still there. I've got staff! He's better off out here with me than in London with strangers. It's a pretty idyllic life. He's got his little friend Georges, he gets to play outside all day, it's expanding his universe, and we get to be together!

*(**JOHN**'s still looking shocked and critical.)*

What? I don't take him to Goma or Lualaba. I don't take him out to the mines! I'm not that reckless.

JOHN. What happened to your column?

ALICE. *(Testing.)* What column?

JOHN. My Front Line.

ALICE. My chick reporter lit?

JOHN. I liked it.

ALICE. It was yummy mummy porn.

JOHN. Don't put yourself down! It made me chuckle. Bibs and flak jackets. Hand grenades and handfuls of organic carrot puree – motherhood as a front line – it was quite clever.

ALICE. 'Quite' clever. It served it's purpose while I was stuck at home with Louis. But it wasn't me.

*(**ALICE** meets **JOHN**'s eye. Their old attraction surfacing.)*

When did you last have sex?

JOHN. About six weeks ago.

ALICE. With Emily?

*(**JOHN** nods.)*

JOHN. When did you last have sex?

ALICE. Not since I split with Guy.

JOHN. A year?

ALICE. Fourteen months and sixteen days.

JOHN. That's a long time. For you.

ALICE. For anyone.

(A frisson. They both feel it.)

We said we wouldn't do this again. You wanted to be a good husband...

JOHN. Well I have been. For a good long time –

ALICE. *(Teasing – sort of.)* How do you live with yourself?

JOHN. How do you?

ALICE. I'm not betraying my wife.

JOHN. No, but aren't you betraying the sisterhood.

ALICE. Ouch.

JOHN. Sorry – did that hurt.

ALICE. Did you want it to?

(The sexual tension has ramped up.)

Selective morality!

JOHN. It's in the job description. You need a conscience to find a story, you need to shelve that conscience to sell it.

*(**ALICE** raises an eyebrow at **JOHN**.)*

ALICE. War junky.

JOHN. It's my profession.

ALICE. It's your drug.

JOHN. And yours!

(Beat. They both know what feels inevitable –)

ALICE. Are you sure you still want to have sex with me now I'm a mother?

(It's clear he does but he holds off.)

(Indicating her breasts.) They fed Louis. I'm a mess of stretch marks – I'm not the same –

JOHN. We should finish washing your head.

> (**ALICE** *puts her finger to her wound. Meets* **JOHN**'*s eye, lowers it with fresh wet blood on it. Holds it out to him.*)
>
> (**JOHN** *looks at it. Hesitates. It's a challenge.*)
>
> (**JOHN** *takes her hand, opens his mouth and sucks her finger clean. They kiss.*)
>
> (**HOPE** *winks at us and draws the curtain to give them a bit of privacy – then pulling on her headphones she starts dancing –*)
>
> (*We hear what she is listening to – as she dances and the scene changes to –*)

Scene Seven – Hackney, London – Council Flat. 27th Floor –

(**KASAMBAYI** *sings loudly along to her iPhone which blares out Congolese Gospel Music. Big energy. Easy presence. She sings at the top of her voice along with the congregation, stopping occasionally to make sure she's in time with them...*)

(*She wears the same brightly coloured African cloth wrapped around her waist that she wrapped around her head, and a Primark T-shirt. She has a huge plastic bucket in front of her on the floor and is bent over it. As she sings she makes beignets. Mixing together flour and water and sugar to make small round doughnut balls ready to deep fat fry. She exudes fierce goodwill.*)

(**HOPE**, *bumps a double buggy into the flat. It has one sleeping baby in it,* **GEORGES**. *She is singing, headphones on. She dumps a plastic picnic box on the side.*)

(*Mother and daughter are completely in their own worlds. Could be occupying two different spaces. Totally ignore each other.* **HOPE** *dumps a backpack and pushes the buggy and sleeping baby into the back room.*)

(**KASAMBAYI** *takes a plastic picnic box out of the backpack and opens it, curious. She lifts out a couple of rice cakes, some carrot sticks, a pack of raisins and some organic mango biscuits. She makes a disapproving grunt.*)

(**HOPE** *dances back in. She's in leggings now.
A tiny top. Pulls on a dressing gown and
slippers. Sexy. Relaxed. With attitude. On the
phone.*)

HOPE. *(Into phone, London street accent.)* No way. No. I'm
not prepared for that. I'm not doing that. He's a sad
skank head who can't sort his life out. Just cos I've got
a kid he thinks I'll mother him and put up with his shit
too. Hang on –

(**HOPE** *flicks out of one call and onto another.
Now she has a French/African/London
accent.*)

Celeste. Mais oui. Deux heures tops.

He's having a nap. Get the documents. I can use the
library. Scan! You'll need a passport photo as well.

(**HOPE** *switches calls again. This time She
puts on a well spoken English middle-class
accent. It tumbles out as naturally as the
others. She's a chameleon. She takes up two
picture books* The Very Hungry Caterpillar
and Dinosaurs and All That Rubbish.*)

Hi Alice. I dropped Louis with his dad. Forgot to give
him the library books. He loved the cucumber and the
mango. Couldn't get him to nap though. Speak soon.

(**KASAMBAYI** *looks to* **HOPE**, *lifts up the
Tupperware showing the rice cakes and
raisins – critical –*)

KASAMBAYI. Bird food. Baby needs milk. Full fat!

(**HOPE** *shakes her head at her mum and ignores
her. Starts doing her hair and make-up.*)

You coming to church?

HOPE. Can't. Helping Celeste with her appeal.

KASAMBAYI. What are they asking her for?

HOPE. Proof of party membership.

KASAMBAYI. Don't get mixed up in the politics.

HOPE. I'm not. I'm just helping her. Like people helped you when you came over! She's got her second hearing coming up. If she doesn't find the proof she'll get sent back.

KASAMBAYI. Don't get into trouble.

HOPE. People helped you. What would you have done without the community.

KASAMBAYI. I am just saying.

HOPE. I thought you'd be proud of me.

KASAMBAYI. Be careful. You know what happened to Pasteur Patrice.

HOPE. He was a big fish. He's a famous preacher.

KASAMBAYI. They murdered him. Here. In England. Poisoned! For being a combattant de la liberté!

(**HOPE** *crosses herself.*)

HOPE. Mum – chill! I'm just trying to help a friend get her papers.

KASAMBAYI. You want to help? Go back to school and finish your education! Get qualifications. Be a lawyer. Be a doctor. Get a degree!

(**HOPE** *glares at her mum sticks in her headphones. Starts dancing provocatively.*)

(**KASAMBAYI** *stares at her a moment. Then clicks off her phone, rips the headphones off* **HOPE.** *She takes an envelope off the side and shoves it into* **HOPE***'s hand.*)

HOPE. What is this?

KASAMBAYI. Girls back home would do anything to have the education you've thrown away. You have no idea how lucky you are.

(**HOPE** *opens the envelope. Shakes her head.*)

This college is recommended by Mr Martin. He can put in a word and write references. He says he can give you extra lessons on top.

HOPE. You went and spoke to my old deputy head teacher? Behind my back?

KASAMBAYI. He's willing to help you. You should be so lucky! Go back to school! Don't let yourself down!

HOPE. How am I letting myself down Mum? How? I'm a mother. A good mum. I've got myself a really good job. I've got a gorgeous son. I'm doing OK!

KASAMBAYI. You were a scholarship girl. You were an A star student. You had a future.

HOPE. I still do! Why can't you be proud of me for Georges!

KASAMBAYI. You could earn a proper living. Take charge of your own life. Be independent.

HOPE. I am independent. I do just what I like.

KASAMBAYI. Who keeps the roof over your head?

HOPE. Give me a chance. I'm nineteen!

KASAMBAYI. You could have got yourself a house. A job. Security.

HOPE. I still can!

KASAMBAYI. I gave you everything and You just did what every uneducated girl does. Got pregnant!

(*Beat. The room is hot and zinging with tension.*)

HOPE. Maybe this was my choice. Maybe being a single mum and dropping out of school is exactly what I wanted!

KASAMBAYI. Mr Martin said you were one of his top students. One of his best ever.

HOPE. I was.

KASAMBAYI. They all had high hopes for you.

HOPE. What is a high hope?

KASAMBAYI. They wanted the best.

HOPE. This IS the best thing that ever happened to me. Georges is the best thing.

KASAMBAYI. What did I do wrong?

HOPE. You didn't.

KASAMBAYI. Why did you go off the rails?

HOPE. To find my own path!

KASAMBAYI. Drugs? Sex?

HOPE. I don't do drugs. I smoked weed. A bit. And I had sex with Georges' father. I haven't had a boyfriend since!

KASAMBAYI. I wanted more for you.

HOPE. More than what? I have freedom. I have the vote. I have food. I have a roof over my head. I have a job. I'm raising my son in safety. It's all good compared to what you had.

KASAMBAYI. I failed you!

HOPE. Stop saying that. I like my life. I'm so grateful to you for all you've done for me. Now you know what – you need to do something for you. Something that makes you happy. Stop living it through me. Do your own A levels!

KASAMBAYI. You're a good girl. And you're a good mum.

HOPE. Thank you.

KASAMBAYI. But you're proud. I know it's hard to admit you've made a mistake/

HOPE. Mum!? Georges is not a mistake! He's a choice!

KASAMBAYI. You had ambitions./

HOPE. And I still do! Just because I have a kid doesn't mean I can't have a career.

KASAMBAYI. I'll give up my job. I'll look after him for you if you'll go back to college.

HOPE. Thank you. But I don't want you to look after my son – I want to look after him myself! If I want to study more I'll go back when the time is right.

(**HOPE** *hesitates for the first time. It's exhausting.*)

KASAMBAYI. Mr Martin is happy to help. He said the school invested in you. He says they still have a vested interest.

HOPE. A vested interest?

KASAMBAYI. He says a lot of people placed a lot of hope in you. The board. The staff. The head. They care.

HOPE. Yes they care. But not about me. They're a business. They're not a community school. They pretend to care but it's all about publicity, results and money. They never cared about me, they cared about their investment. It wasn't good for them when I dropped out, their one black scholarship pupil! I was there to shore up their guilt – my picture on the front of the prospectus let those middle class mums kid themselves they were sending their white privilege kids to a diverse school. I was ALL the black diversity in my year, do you know that?!

KASAMBAYI. You're twisting things.

HOPE. No. I'm untwisting them.

KASAMBAYI. Why do you feel the need to see it that way?

HOPE. Because it is that way.

>*(Beat.)*

I wish I'd never got a scholarship. I wish I'd never gone to that school. That's what sent me off the rails. There was no one like me there. I didn't belong. I was just there as a 'sticking plaster' for the social conscience of the white middle class.

>*(**KASAMBAYI** makes a disapproving noise –)*

It's true.

>*(**HOPE** heads to the mirror – starts doing her make-up.)*

KASAMBAYI. What does your new friend Alice think? I bet she had an education. I bet she got her degree. What does she think of your choices?

HOPE. Georges is the making of me. That's what Alice says. Not an A star in a 'dead language' to please my investors!

KASAMBAYI. That's not fair.

HOPE. It's equal. I'm being equal. You just don't like what you're hearing. You don't want to hear it. Trust me mum. Alice trusts me. Why can't you?

>*(**KASAMBAYI** takes up her phone – flashes it at **HOPE**. A picture of **ALICE** – a review of her book* My Front Line.*)*

KASAMBAYI. "Alice Young's New Front Line!"

(**KASAMBAYI** *throws another newspaper down* - **ALICE***'s portrait on the front -)*

"Front Line Correspondent Alice Young toughs it out on her new front line..." She's a fraud! Why are you looking after her baby? You could be writing your own book!

HOPE. She's not a fraud – she was kidnapped once. It was on the news – it took weeks to negotiate her release – She's a really good journalist. I've been reading her work for her. I've started proofing her stuff. It's really interesting. I'm learning. She respects me!

(*Beat –)*

She wants to up my salary and my work hours. She wants me to be her assistant. She's asked me to travel with her to help with her work and to look after Louis on her next trip.

KASAMBAYI. Where?

HOPE. Congo.

(*Tiny beat. But fierce and ringing.)*

KASAMBAYI. Where?

(*But* **KASAMBAYI***'s heard.* **HOPE** *knows she's dropped a bomb. Mother and daughter stare at each other.)*

HOPE. She's writing about Cobalt mining in Katanga.

She's going out for a few months, she needs an assistant and she doesn't want to leave Louis behind so...

KASAMBAYI. You can't go.

HOPE. I want to see where I come from.

KASAMBAYI. You are not going.

HOPE. I'll be looked after. Alice has been loads. She stays in hotels and stuff. Gated communities. Old colonial houses. Not dangerous places like where you lived. She's shown me pictures.

> (**KASAMBAYI** *cries out. As if she's been winded. Sinks onto the sofa.* **HOPE** *is shocked. Afraid suddenly.*)

KASAMBAYI. No!

HOPE. I told Alice you came from Congo. I told her I speak some Lingala.

> (**KASAMBAYI** *is rocking on the sofa.*)

It's OK mum. It's really exciting. I can find out who I am. Where I come from. Maybe I can even find someone who knew Dad. I'll be fine I promise.

> (*The lights go down on* **KASAMBAYI.** **HOPE** *is left alone – light rises on another part of the stage revealing –*)

Scene Eight – Hotel Room. Lubumbashi, Congo
Present Day –

(**ALICE** and **JOHN** *lie postcoital in each others arms – it's dark outside now. Occasional car lights flash across the room. A sickly street light glows.*)

(**HOPE** *watches them – grows impatient – Like a child she pokes them awake – then moves away to watch from the sidelines.*)

JOHN. I've missed you.

ALICE. I've missed you too.

(*A beat as* **ALICE** *takes it all in –*)

ALICE. I've missed it all!

I've been desperate to get back out.

JOHN. What stopped you?

(**ALICE** *almost laughs – what doesn't* **JOHN** *understand.*)

ALICE. I asked for a meeting with Alistair when Louis was about two months. I was mid-pitch, and suddenly my milk came in. Like a tap. Two wet patches. He has four kids but he went all embarrassed and disapproving. Was I sure I was ready?

JOHN. Two months is little. Were you?

(**ALICE** *shoots* **JOHN** *a look.*)

ALICE. I asked Guy to travel with me. To help.

JOHN. Did he?

(**ALICE** *shakes her head.*)

ALICE. He said I was mad.

> (**JOHN** *nods his head knowingly.*)

Would you have?

> (**JOHN***'s hesitation says it all.*)

I'm not the first foreign correspondent to take their kid to work you know. Martha Gelhorn did it. Victoria Brittain took her son out to Vietnam, and cycled round with him in the basket on her bicycle. Her kids have done really well. It didn't fuck them up.

JOHN. So what happened? Did you go?

ALICE. No. I called the editor and said I was taking a bit more maternity leave.

JOHN. How is Guy with Louis. Is he enjoying fatherhood?

ALICE. I didn't tell him I was pregnant until it was too late to terminate. He was pretty upset. Felt cheated. Said it was his decision too – but I didn't want to be persuaded to abort again –

> (**ALICE** *eyeballs* **JOHN**. *History there.*)

Our baby would have been five now.

JOHN. It wasn't a baby.

ALICE. I know. And I am violently pro abortion. But I also know that I chose to end something.

I saw the foetus on the screen. They have to locate it so they know where to suction. I saw it's heart beating – it didn't stop me.

> (*Beat. They both let this settle.*)

Thing is Guy and I never really liked each other. Pretty soon he had an affair. I could smell it. Seamed in there alongside the cigarettes and the sweat and the sterile hotel air. Some young reporter. Girl. Young, strong, free. Like I used to be.

JOHN. You're still young and strong.

ALICE. But I'm not a girl and I'm not free. Anyway. I threw him out. And I walked.

JOHN. Walked?

ALICE. Regents Park, Kew Gardens, Hyde Park, Ally Pally, London Fields, Hackney Marshes, Hampstead Heath, Greenwich, London Parks. Crossing London. I think maybe I was having a kind of breakdown – post natal desperation. I just had to keep moving. If I stopped I panicked.

(Off **JOHN** laughing.)

I took a diary with me and wrote and noted. It was amazing. Eye-opening. There's a whole subculture of mums and grannies and nannies in parks. I'd never noticed before. And that's when I had the idea for it – pushing him on the swings – listening to a granny explain what hard work Terry Towelling nappies were and how we have it so easy now – "My Front Line"

JOHN. Emily loved it.

ALICE. Course she did! I gave her first world moans traction! Comparing the bomb site of a playroom to the bomb-ripped cities of Syria.

JOHN. What's wrong with that? It's a tough job!

ALICE. Since when are you an expert?

JOHN. I've raised four kids Alice.

ALICE. Emily raised them. You were hardly ever there.

JOHN. That's not fair –

ALICE. On who? Them or you?

(Tense silence. Has she gone too far?)

JOHN. Emily isn't like you. Emily didn't want to work. Emily was happy devoting herself to the children.

*(**ALICE** considers attacking this – decides not to –)*

ALICE. Did she actually say that? Or is that your interpretation?

(Beat.)

It's a bloody hard job. You should try it. You're at the front line of the creation of a human being and there is nothing more important or more demanding than that. Nothing which takes more selflessness.

JOHN. I think you found your voice. That column is a fine piece of writing. Don't knock it. It's hard to mother and be on the road.

ALICE. What are you saying?

JOHN. Kids need stability. They need roots.

ALICE. I'm his roots.

JOHN. I think your column could be a great book –

ALICE. You want me to potter round the playgroups and write in the evenings?

JOHN. I don't want you to be or do anything. I'm just saying.

ALICE. Did you ever spend a full day alone looking after your kids?

*(**JOHN** considers doesn't confirm or deny.)*

Try spending a few months alone with only a pre-verbal toddler as your main companion. Try listening daily to Mum's obsessing about their kids tantrums as if they've survived some natural disaster, or some pampered

Putney princess confiding about her cosmetic tucks to tidy her labia and arsehole post birth. I wanted to scream – "There is more than this. There's a whole world out there beyond these playgroups and nappies and tottering toddlers" *And at the same time feeling.* "No. This is all there is. This exact moment in Louis' life is all that matters because these are the building blocks of his whole self and he's got to be happy and loved." Already he's got no dad. He's not likely to have a sibling. I've got to be here for him.

> (**JOHN** *pulls her towards him. She pulls away. Still more to say –)*

I finally managed to go away. Syria. Four weeks. And it was awful. I missed him so much – like an amputation.

I was desperate by the time I got back. mum was there, Louis asleep in his buggy. Soft face. Lips. Curls. "How is he?" I asked and he must have heard my voice because he opened his eyes. I spoke again and his eyes opened wider as if he couldn't quite believe what he was hearing. And then he turned his head and looked up at me. Just looked up at me. Still. And I looked back at him and smiled. Felt my smile stretching through every alive part of me, And then he started to tremble. I looked at mum worried. She to me. I bent down and undid the buggy and he was still trembling. No tears. No crying. Just trembling. He took my hand, led me to the bookshelf, took a book and gave it to me still shaking. So I spoke to him, and kissed him, but he just gave me the book and took me to the sofa and sat beside me and shook and trembled and looked from me to the book and the book to me. I read it to him. And he still sat there, and I realised that he had thought I was gone forever. Gone forever. That is what I had done to him.

I knew I could never leave him again until he could understand.

*(**JOHN** gathers a tear from **ALICE**'s cheek with his finger and licks it. They kiss.)*

Why are tears sexy for you?? What is it? Some kind of deep rooted power thing?

JOHN. That's so fucked up.

ALICE. No it's honest. *(She puts her hand on his groin.)* And you're hard!

*(They kiss. Then **ALICE** pulls away.)*

JOHN. There are stories you could tell, without having to travel. Louis needs you alive. How about the human cost of Cobalt. The child labour. Or write about the East – you've researched it enough, you've got enough material – the raped and abused women.

ALICE. People don't want a Sunday supplement about rape. They don't want their roast violated by fistulas. Rape doesn't get coverage. But Cobalt is sexy. Cobalt sells. As a mineral and a story.

*(Beat. **ALICE** lies back. **JOHN** takes up his camera. He frames her – takes a picture of her.)*

JOHN. My muse.

ALICE. I'm nobody's muse. I'm Alice. I'm Louis' mum.

*(**JOHN** takes another few photos. **ALICE** ignores it. Keeps talking.)*

*(**HOPE** who has been watching all this time moves back into focus under the following.)*

There's some psychic umbilical cord that connects us and our moods. If I'm happy so is he. He's flourishing out here. He makes it possible for me.

I love coming back to him and Georges and Hope curled on the sofa. She's a big sister to him and a little sister to me. I love the smell of her and Georges on Louis when I hold him. We've all started to smell and feel the same. Like a family.

JOHN. You smell of sex to me.

> *(They kiss. He lies back and she straddles him.)*

ALICE. Do you want more?

JOHN. Who knows when the next time will be?

ALICE. You'll never going to leave her are you?

JOHN. Would you want me to?

ALICE. I don't know. Sometimes I think being lovers is the best option. We get all the best times none of the worst.

> *(They look at each other.)*

Other times I can't help wishing that we'd just gone for it and Louis was yours.

> *(**JOHN** rolls **ALICE** onto her back. He gets off the bed onto his knees and pulls her towards him, goes to kiss her between her legs. **ALICE** pulls back, hesitates.)*

Louis was big. I tore.

> *(**JOHN** starts stroking **ALICE**'s legs encouraging her to open them. She still fights to hold them together.)*

No one's kissed me there since he was born.

JOHN. I need to feel you come. Please.

> *(**JOHN** strokes **ALICE**'s thighs. Gently opens her legs. She allows it. Lies back. **JOHN** starts to bury his head between her legs.)*

(*Suddenly* **ALICE**'s *mobile buzzes. They ignore it. It keeps buzzing.*)

(**HOPE** *picks up the mobile and holds it out to* **ALICE** – *watches* – *intrigued.*)

ALICE. Hang on. Sorry.

(**ALICE** *takes the phone from* **HOPE**, *not seeing her.*)

Hello?

(*She freezes. Some presentiment.*)

Hello? Yes, speaking. What is it? Please. What's happened? I need to know.

(*A beat. A tiny whimper escapes her.*)

Oh God. Thank you. I'm on my way.

(**ALICE** *hangs up. She's wired.*)

JOHN. What? What is it?

(**ALICE** *can't speak.*)

Alice? What's happened.

ALICE. There's been a shooting. On the farm.

(**ALICE** *stands frozen. Her world falling apart.*)

Scene Nine – Nowhere – Anywhere – Everywhere –

(**HOPE** *moves into the centre of the light – or the light finds her.*)

HOPE. The closest I have ever felt to death, except when I actually died – was when I gave birth to Georges.

The agony of it. The complete commitment of it. Nothing observed, everything suffered. Everything in me so totally committed to one thing. Brain; heart; past; future; present; lungs; breath. All ripping me open. And then Georges on my chest. Warm, heavy, slippery. Alive. Arrived.

And this thought went through me in the post euphoric soup of hormones and endorphins and relief. If this is Alive. Arrived. Then dying, departing can be no better or worse. No less wondrous. No much less or more of a battle. No much less or more of a commitment.

And I was right. Death is just birth. Backwards. It's as much of a struggle getting out of this world as it is getting into it.

Proposed Interval

ACT TWO

(The verandah of an old colonial Edwardian house. Deep in the Congolese bush.)

*(**ALICE** places a record on the gramophone. Ave Maria – sung by choir boys.)*

*(A teenage girl **MERCY** [played by **HOPE**]. Comes in drawing with a stick on a leaf, copying a text. The stick scratches the leaves leaving clear red marks. A slate made by nature.)*

MERCY. Who is singing?

ALICE. Boys. English boys. Younger than you. Choir boys.

MERCY. Where?

ALICE. In England. In a beautiful cathedral, a building where we go to worship God. As tall as the tallest trees in the forest but made out of stone. Their voices were recorded. They are praising Mary, Mother of God.

MERCY. You said Mary was the Mother of Jesus?

ALICE. Yes. Jesus is God's son.

MERCY. How can she be Mother of God and Wife of God at the same time?

(**ALICE** *hesitates – stumped.*)

Is she a witch?

ALICE. No of course not Mercy? What on earth made you think that?

MERCY. She lay with God.

ALICE. She didn't lie with God. What happened. In the Christian church we call it a miracle.

MERCY. We call that a witch.

> (**ALICE** *lays the table. Huntley and Palmers biscuits. China cups.*)

ALICE. These were my grandmothers' tea cups. My mother handworked this tablecloth for us just before we left.

> (**MERCY** *shows* **ALICE** *her finished writing on the leaf.*)

MERCY. "Lord Save Me"

ALICE. Excellent Mercy. That is the shortest prayer in God's book.

MERCY. God wrote a book?

ALICE. *The Bible* is God's book. His disciples, his followers, wrote it for him.

MERCY. Why? Can't God write?

ALICE. Well – God himself doesn't need to write. You don't need to write in Heaven. Our Saviour Jesus could write. But he died before he could write his story. So his followers provided testimony for him.

MERCY. Will your Saviour help us?

ALICE. If we pray to him. I believe he will.

May I take a photograph of you holding your work? I would like to send my children in London a picture of my children out here.

(**ALICE** *takes up her Kodak camera.*)

Perfect.

MERCY. How does it work?

ALICE. Whatever you see in the square, when you push the button and make the flash, the camera will catch that picture – forever.

MERCY. You are very clever at catching things to keep.

ALICE. How do you mean?

MERCY. Voices. (*Pointing to the gramophone.*) People. (*Pointing to the camera.*)

(**ALICE** *takes out of a box the framed picture of her two children Freddie and Katherine.*)

ALICE. These are my children. This is Freddie. And this is Katherine.

MERCY. Is she sad?

ALICE. I don't think so.

(*But* **ALICE** *scrutinises the photo in a new way.*)

MERCY. Why don't they come here with you?

ALICE. How could I do my work here and support John and teach you to read if I had my own children to look after too? A missionary wife must serve God first and her husband second. That is my duty. And my vocation.

MERCY. Who looks after them?

ALICE. They are in a big happy building called Marley House, with lots of other children whose parents are

working all over the world spreading Gods word.
There's a lady called Auntie May who looks after them.
A school for mission children.

> (**MERCY** *eyes the sugar on the table. She
> catches* **ALICE***'s eye.*)

Just one.

> (**MERCY** *carefully takes a sugar lump and
> licks it.*)

MERCY. We have to supply all the food for the force
publique. Last week they ate all our manioc and
sugarcane. We had nothing left for us. This week we
must find more supplies for them. What we grow is
now for the Belgians.

> (*Suddenly they look up – coming out of the
> bush, exhausted, weary, haunted –* **JOHN** *and
> a little group carrying bags.*)

> (**ALICE** *runs to meet* **JOHN**. *Sweaty, haggard,
> dirty.*)

ALICE. John? You're back!

> (**JOHN** *collapses at the table.*)

JOHN. Lord Save Me.

> (*A giggle of excited recognition spirals up
> from* **MERCY**. **JOHN** *raises his head confused.*
> **ALICE** *understands.*)

ALICE. Mercy – show Mr Harris your work.

> (**MERCY** *shyly show her leaf to* **JOHN**. *"Lord
> Save Me" shines out in red juice. He forces
> himself to be encouraging…*)

JOHN. You know whose prayer that is? St Peter's. He was one of Jesus' disciples. Jesus taught him to walk on water.

MERCY. You can't walk on water.

JOHN. Exactly. Peter knew that. So he was terrified. He was sure he'd be swallowed up and drowned. He stepped out onto the waves of a huge expanse of water called the sea, and as he did he cried out "Lord Save Me" thinking he was going to die – but the Lord caused the waters to hold him up and he did walk on water. So that is the prayer that asks for a miracle. *(To himself and* **ALICE***.)* And a miracle is what we need now.

> *(***JOHN*** collapses again.* **ALICE** *ushers* **MERCY** *out.)*

ALICE. What is it John?

JOHN. Prayers are not enough. I am not equipped.

ALICE. What happened?

JOHN. Why did we come here? Please. Remind me.

ALICE. *(Scared.)* John?

> *(***JOHN*** says nothing – stares ahead. Shakes.)*

We don't have to stay here John. There's no shame in returning home.

> *(***JOHN*** can't find words –* **ALICE** *pushes on –)*

I've been struggling too –

> *(***JOHN*** looks up at her as if he doesn't understand.)*

When I gave birth to our children I also gave birth to a new powerful vocation – to serve them. And these two vocations, to serve God and to serve them battle in me now.

*(Now **JOHN** is listening, as if the word "God" re-engages him, cut through, clarifies things.)*

JOHN. Do our children have a roof over their head Alice?

ALICE. Yes.

JOHN. Do they lack food? Do they lack companionship? Do they lack education?

ALICE. No John.

JOHN. Then what do they lack?

ALICE. Maybe they lack love? A mother's love.

JOHN. We have spoken about this Alice. I thought we agreed. They have God's love. They will know you in time.

ALICE. I thought I could do this John. I wanted to. But I can't.

(Beat. Of judgement.)

JOHN. I have always said I would not stand in your way. If you want to return you must. But I can't return with you.

We have walked into a trap.

ALICE. What do you mean?

JOHN. King Leopold is manipulating God's word to serve the devil. He is using the scriptures, and missionaries like us who spread the word, to serve a purpose God never intended!

We are being used to silence and control. To encourage the people to submit to suffering. We are being used to doctrinate them – so that they will accept being exploited and degraded and abused! We are being used to collude in the most horrific atrocities. What is happening here is beyond imagination.

ALICE. What have you seen?

JOHN. The men climb the trees to cut down the rubber vines for the sap. Half-famished and bone weary. Their wives and children are kept locked up in boiling huts until they return, and if they fail to collect their daily quota they are starved, or...

(He hesitates he can't go on...)

ALICE. What did you see?

JOHN. We saw baskets full of smoked human hands.

Preserved to take back to the overseers as proof that they have punished the workers families. They cut peoples hands off while they are still alive to save expenditure on bullets.

ALICE. Oh John.

JOHN. I have seen the invisible worm. We are in the centre of Blakes Rose. The dark secret love is the 'greed' of King Leopold, the greed of the world to possess the rubber wheels that carry capitalism forward.

I can't go home Alice. God sent me here. Not to spread his word – but to defeat the white man and hold him to account.

*(**JOHN** rises and heads inside leaving **ALICE** alone.)*

*(Suddenly **MERCY** comes hurrying onto the stage. It is clear something is the matter. She looks scared.)*

ALICE. What's the matter? What is it?

*(**MERCY** looks towards a man **NSALA** heading to the house very slowly, carrying a small parcel wrapped in a plantain leaf. There is something apart about him, as if he is carrying a ghost.)*

MERCY. Nsala asks he has something to give you.

> (**ALICE** *looks towards the young man approaching. She brushes down her skirts. Rises, formal.*)

ALICE. Good afternoon Nsala.

> (**NSALA** *says nothing. Just holds out the parcel.* **ALICE** *takes it.*)

Thank you. Very much. Shall I open it?

> (**NSALA** *nods.*)

> (**ALICE** *carefully opens the parcel.*)

> (*She gasps. She almost drops the parcel. In horror. With her we see two tiny pieces of human anatomy –*)

> (*– A tiny child's foot, a tiny hand.*)

MERCY. This is the hand and foot of Boali. His daughter. She is five years old.

> (**ALICE** *stares aghast.*)

ALICE. I am so sorry Nsala. What happened?

MERCY. He didn't make his rubber quota for the day. The overseers did this. Then they killed her. But they weren't finished. Then they killed his wife too.

> (*There is total silence. What is there to say?*)

> (**NSALA** *sits on the verandah. Carefully, tenderly, he lays out his little bundle. He nods to* **ALICE**.)

ALICE. What can I do?

MERCY. He wants you to take his picture. He wants you to send it to your King. He wants him to see what is happening here and to stop it.

*(***ALICE*** *nods to* ***NSALA***. *Slow, reverential almost, she takes up her camera.)*

*(***NSALA*** *sits on the verandah. Exactly as he does in the photograph that exists to this day.)*

*(***ALICE*** *frames the shot. The camera flashes. The lights go black.)*

(When they come up the real photo taken by ***ALICE*** *one hundred years ago – just staged – is the backdrop.)*

Scene Two – A London Morgue. Present Day –

(*A* **MORGUE ASSISTANT** *in a white coat wheels on a trolley with a body on it. The body is covered with a white cloth.*)

(**KASAMBAYI** *follows. At a first glance she looks as if she's working in the morgue too. She's wearing a white plastic apron. She carries a large bag.*)

(*The* **MORGUE ASSISTANT** *heads out and returns wheeling in another trolley. On this one is a large bowl of water, a jug, a comb, scissors, disinfectant, soap, cloths and towels and wipes for cleaning.*)

ASSISTANT.   Can we get you anything else?

(**KASAMBAYI** *shakes her head.*)

Please ring if you need assistance.

(*The* **ASSISTANT** *heads out. The door clicks.*)

(**KASAMBAYI** *stands totally still. Absolutely silent. She closes her eyes.*)

(*She opens them again. She walks over to the trolley and pulls back the sheet. To reveal Hope nineteen, in a plain white hospital robe.*)

(**KASAMBAYI** *folds back the sheet. She is practised, technical, professional.*)

(*She takes the bowl of water. Starts to clean Hope's body.*)

(A knock. The door opens abruptly. **ALICE** *stands there. She freezes in shock seeing Hope's corpse.)*

*(***KASAMBAYI*** *freezes seeing* **ALICE**.*)*

ALICE. Oh my God. They said the body was ready.

*(***KASAMBAYI*** *stands and stares.)*

How long will it take do you think?

*(***KASAMBAYI*** *stands and stares.)*

What time shall I come back?

*(***KASAMBAYI*** *stands and stares.)*

Do you speak English?

*(***KASAMBAYI*** *stands and stares.)*

Jesus. This is all I need. OK. I'll find someone don't worry.

*(***ALICE*** *goes to leave.)*

KASAMBAYI. *(Very quietly.)* Alice Young.

*(***ALICE*** *spins back round. Meets* **KASAMBAYI**'*s eyes again. Suddenly it all makes sense.)*

ALICE. Mrs Mabele?

(Beat.)

ALICE. I am so sorry. I am so sorry. I – (**ALICE** *chokes, can't go on.)*

*(***KASAMBAYI*** *waits, doesn't move. Stares at* **ALICE**. **ALICE** *finally raises her head. Ashamed.)*

Is there anything I can do to help?

(**KASAMBAYI** *doesn't answer. She turns back to Hope and continues washing her. After a while she starts talking. As if to herself.*)

KASAMBAYI. When she was little as soon as she could hold a piece of soap and a flannel she insisted on washing herself. She was so quick and bright. She never wanted me to do anything for her. Her spirit was independent right from the start. Independent and restless. She never belonged to me. Even as a baby. She was not like my other children.

ALICE. I thought she was an only child?

KASAMBAYI. She had two older brothers.

ALICE. She never talked about them.

KASAMBAYI. No. What you don't know about you can't speak about.

(**ALICE** *hesitates. How to process this.*)

(**KASAMBAYI** *takes Hope's hand up, starts cleaning it.*)

This is her father's hand. I used to find it hard to hold her hand even when she was little – because I found him there.

He had a strange crooked little finger and a flat thumb like a spade. I know his hand. I found it again...

(*She addresses Hope now.*)

Every time I held your hand to cross a road, to teach you to hold a pen, to high five you – I held your father's hand too.

I wasn't always good to you. You tore me two ways. It wasn't always easy for me to love you. But I did my best.

(**ALICE** *is silent, listening – says nothing. Encourages more.*)

Georges has his hands too. So you see I cannot forget. He is still with me. The Lord does not want me to forget. He forces me daily to love what I would hate.

ALICE. I thought her father was killed by the rebels.

KASAMBAYI. No. Her father was the rebel who killed my husband and her brothers, and cut off my hand, and raped me.

ALICE. She never said.

KASAMBAYI. She never knew. I didn't burden her with that.

I suffered enough. And my suffering bore fruit.

You see, you can do the worst things to a woman and she can still bless you. It is our nature: our blessing, and our curse.

They did the worst things to me but I changed those things to love. To my Hope.

> (*Beat.* **KASAMBAYI** *turns to* **ALICE**. *Accusing. Calm. Demolishing.*)

You should never have taken her to Congo. You should have asked me first.

You had no right to take her back to the land of her ancestors. No right.

ALICE. I'm sorry.

KASAMBAYI. You are blind Mrs Young. You call yourself a journalist. You travel the world to find your answers – when the story you needed was staring you in the face right there. Right beside you on your own doorstep.

> (**KASAMBAYI** *turns to Hope. Strokes her hand. Takes it up.*)

(*To Hope gentle.*) What happened?

(She raises her head to **ALICE***.)*

What happened?

ALICE. We don't know. The foreign office are still looking into exactly what took place. There was a limited police report. They should have sent it to you.

KASAMBAYI. It told me nothing.

ALICE. They haven't been able to find her...attackers yet.

KASAMBAYI. You surprise me.

ALICE. I promise you. We will find those responsible!

KASAMBAYI. I hold you responsible.

> *(***KASAMBAYI*** *stares at* **ALICE***.* **ALICE** *freezes. Can't respond.)*

I knew. When she told me she was going away with you. I knew. I felt her ending.

You – are responsible for her death Mrs Young!

> *(***ALICE*** *can say nothing.)*

Come. See!

> *(***ALICE*** *still stands back.* **KASAMBAYI** *takes her by the arm and guides her forward.)*

I don't need a police report. It is written on her body. They have tidied her but I can read the story.

See where they shot her. Three times. One. Two. And three – there.

> *(***ALICE*** *suddenly turns and vomits – grabs up the water bowl just in time and throws up in it.* **KASAMBAYI** *watches her.)*

What were you doing – letting a vulnerable English girl run riot around Kinshasa?

Did you even ask where she was going? Did you even check up on her?

ALICE. She had weekends off. It was her free time. I didn't make it my business.

KASAMBAYI. *(To* **ALICE**.*)* You should have made it your business.

ALICE. She said she knew people. I assumed they were family –

KASAMBAYI. Assumed!!! She has no family in Kinshasa. Her family – my family – were from East Congo. And they were all killed. No one left for her to find.

She was nineteen. A child! In your care!

What happened?

What happened?

> *(**ALICE** swallows. Forces herself to push on.)*

ALICE. The Police went through her diary and her phone. It seems she got in some kind of a relationship with a young, local journalist: a bit of a firebrand.

She invited him round to the farm when I was away one weekend. He was followed. They must have bribed the guard at the gate. It must have got heated. Maybe she tried to protect him. All we know is they shot them.

> *(**KASAMBAYI** goes to Hope. She takes her daughter's hand.)*

KASAMBAYI. Everything I tried to protect you from, you found. I locked it away but it found you. It happened again. The same. Only I survived. You died.

I prayed for death but I didn't get it. I couldn't get life either. Until I had you.

> *(**KASAMBAYI** holds Hope's hand to her mouth and kisses it.)*

Now I will hold your son's hand. Be free. I will look after him for you.

> (**KASAMBAYI** *draws Hope up to standing. Makes her a head dress from the same Congolese cloth that bandaged her head on the bus in scene one – the cloth that was baby Hope.*)

You look beautiful. You are beautiful. You are. Now you will meet my husband and your brothers. They are waiting for you. You are ready.

> (*Hope remains expressionless.* **KASAMBAYI** *leads her out – they walk out holding hands.*)

> (**ALICE** *is left alone.*)

> (*Stillness settles in the space. At last* **ALICE** *turns back to the trolley.*)

> (*Hope still lies on it.*)

> (*Dressed as her mother dressed her. But stone cold dead.*)

> (*The* **MORGUE ASSISTANT** *comes in and nod cursorily to* **ALICE**. *They cover the body with a cloth and they wheel it away.*)

> (**ALICE** *is left standing alone on the stage in a pool of light. In a pool of blood.*)

Scene Three – Continuous. Somewhere. Everywhere. Nowhere –

(**ALICE** *closes her eyes. As she does we hear Hope's voice. Hope comes in and stands by her or behind her during the monologue. She is vibrant and full of life and excitement.*)

HOPE. Do you remember how we first met?

ALICE. I do.

It was the changing room at the swimming pool. It was the babies swimming class. That small pool at Hackney Baths.

HOPE. It was amazing. We had to hold the babies underwater, right under, and they would swim back to the surface.

ALICE. Like putting them back in the womb. They just held their breath and swam right back to their beginning. Into the world for the first time.

HOPE. I remember you had a really sleek black swimming costume, and your long hair. You talked in a really loud assured voice. Posh. But warm.

ALICE. I remember Louis had really cool swimming pants. Pink with blue stars,

HOPE. I wished I had some like that for Georges. I remember thinking you probably lived in one of those huge houses by Victoria Park and had four kids and a husband who came home and loved you every night.

Funny how you can be so wrong.

ALICE. It was the time Louis pooed in the swimming pool at his lesson. The poo popped out of the side of his cool pink trunks with blue stars and floated up to the surface.

LIFEGUARD. Hey what's that?

> (**ALICE** *scoops up the little hard poo in her hand –*)

ALICE. Whoops. Looks like Louis...

LIFEGUARD. Right out everyone. Immediately. Out now please!

> (*An alarm goes off.*)

HOPE. It's was like we'd just found an unexploded bomb. Everyone was shepherded out of the water. An Lifeguards descended with nets and sprays and hoses.

LIFEGUARD. You all have to sign a health and safety form before you leave the building, and you *(to Alice)* can't come back in the pool until he has proper nappy swim pants!

ALICE. We all had to sign a health and safety form. And I was told Louis couldn't come back in the pool without nappy water pants or until he was potty trained.

> (**HOPE** *laughs at the memory.*)

HOPE. You wrote about it later in your column.

You made it funny. But at the time we all just felt really bad and embarrassed for you.

Later I was in the changing room.

> (**HOPE** *is drying between her toes. She coos at* **GEORGES**, *making him giggle and gurgle.*)

ALICE. And I came in. I was kind of tense after everything that had happened. So Louis was tense too. He was red and screaming.

> (**ALICE** *makes* **LOUIS'** *screaming noises as she tries to hush him.*)

HOPE. Georges was dressed and kicking happily. I saw you struggling.

ALICE. I tried to feed him but he was way too caught up in his own howling. The old grannies were giving me critical looks.

It was all going into that spiral of total scream.

> (**HOPE** *comes over.*)

HOPE. Shall I hold him for you while you change?

> (**ALICE**, *desperate, still screaming, passes* **LOUIS** *to* **HOPE**.)

My God would you? Would you mind? Thank you.

> (**ALICE** *watches. As* **HOPE** *calms* **LOUIS**. **ALICE** *calms too.*)

(**HOPE** *addresses the next to the audience -)*A mother's body against a child's body makes a place. It says you are here. Without this body against your body there is no place.

> (**HOPE** *passes the sleeping* **LOUIS** *back to a calm and grateful* **ALICE**.)

ALICE. Thank you. Thank you so much.

HOPE. My pleasure.

I headed off back to the flat. Pushing Georges. Wishing I didn't have to live with my mum.

ALICE. I headed off home, wishing I had someone to share it all with – and suddenly I had an idea –

HOPE. And suddenly I felt a wind at my back and you were there beside me. Your hair was still wet. You had Louis in the buggy I wanted. You had this really cool retro 60's coat.

ALICE. Excuse me. I just wondered. Do you ever do any childminding, because you're amazing with kids. Sorry. I should introduce myself. I'm Alice – Alice Young.

HOPE. I'm Hope

(**ALICE** *heads away holding herself tight.*)

(**HOPE**, *alone, addresses the audience.*)

HOPE. You know when people talk about near death, the white light and the end of the tunnel stuff. I left my body, saw it lying there – do not believe them. Dying isn't dead. I fractured, splintered, and my pain burned red hot, screaming synapses found frequencies, tuned into flocks of other silenced murders still thronging the air.

In my ending I bore witness to the million other endings hovering there – for one brief moment I was everything. And then I wasn't. Because I was gone.

(*And suddenly – she isn't there.*)

Scene Four – Baringa, Congo. Mission House 1903 –

(A table is laid with tea and has on it Alice's photo's wrapped in brown paper. Alice has clearly been looking through them and will be back in a moment. NSALA enters. He comes near the table to wait. He looks down at the table. What he sees inflames him and upsets him. NSALA circles the table – urgent – upset. He stares at the photographs. Suddenly he can't help himself. He takes up the one of himself and his daughter. ALICE comes out, shocked to see NSALA.)

ALICE. Nsala!

(With a pained cry NSALA puts the photo back down. Impassioned.)

NSALA. You take our pictures. You take our stories. You promise to help. But you do nothing!

ALICE. I'm doing all I can.

NSALA. It's not enough.

ALICE. Nsala – have patience. When I return home I will take all this as evidence and speak to the important people in my country. We will hold King Leopold to account for the crimes he has committed I promise you, and for his attempted murder of a nation. In two years.

NSALA. Two years is too long. Now!

(NSALA takes charge. He comes forward. He takes the photos and puts them in the box. He bangs the box down in front of ALICE. He wraps the box with brown paper.)

You see us suffer. You see us die. Do you not see us as people. Do you not see our pain?

*(He shoves the rough package at **ALICE**.)*

Send them. Now!

(She hesitates a moment, then –)

ALICE.   Alright. You're right. We'll send them now. If we hurry we can make the steamer before it leaves tomorrow.

*(**ALICE** heads into the house with **NSALA**.)*

Scene Five – Continuous. Somewhere. Everywhere. Nowhere –

(**HOPE** *moves tentatively forward onto the stage. carries an insect spray and wears sunglasses. She uses the spray to clear the air before she moves forward.*)

(*Cicadas start to chirrup...*)

HOPE. Shall I tell you a secret? I was big time disappointed when I first got to Africa. I guess I hoped going there might help me understand myself. Might help me feel like I belonged. I know it's stupid but I secretly hoped I might find family. People who knew my dad. I wanted it to feel like home. It didn't.

So many bugs. And see through lizards. So you can see their insides and their hearts beating. And the dust – like rust –

I zapped everything everywhere I went.

My body was happy though. It felt more at home than I did. My excema dried up. I stopped using my inhaler.

The weekends I went into Kinshasa alone. I had some numbers Celeste had given me. I met this journalist. David. He took me to the cheetah bar –

(*Low thrumming music.* **HOPE** *is at the bar – can't help moving to the beat – so alive. She takes out a cigarette –* **DAVID** *[twenty five Congolese, strong, fit, fierce, gentle, bit of a swagger] comes over with a drink and lights it for her. There's an attraction between them. They're flirting.*)

What are the lights over the river?

DAVID. Brazzaville.

HOPE. Why are there two Congo's

DAVID. They're two different countries. Congo-Brazzaville was colonised by France. Congo-Kinshasa was colonised by Belgium.

HOPE. That was a bad patch.

DAVID. It's not history.

HOPE. The scramble for Africa?

DAVID. They're still scrambling! Diamonds, Rubber, Copper, Coltan - Cobalt!

We feed the world.

But the global market relies on keeping us hungry. Everything – economic structures, global institutions – it's all designed to keep us exactly where we are. Whether it's Europe, or the US or now China – they need those raw materials and they need them dirt cheap. They don't want their living standards to fall. They'll fight dirty to block any change.

> (**DAVID** *starts swaying with* **HOPE**, *dancing with her. They fit well together. He admires her, comes up with a nickname –)*

Nzala.

HOPE. What's Nzala?

DAVID. You don't know Nzala?

> (**HOPE** *shakes her head – shy of her ignorance.)*

She was a Congolese Queen. She fought the Portuguese in 1640. With a female army. Got them to agree a peace treaty. She was a symbol of a fight against oppression. A Goddess.

HOPE. I'll take it as a compliment then.

DAVID. It's meant as one. *(With a smile.)* Mundele.

HOPE. Mundele?

DAVID. It means a white European style person.

HOPE. I know mundele. I'm black.

DAVID. You talk white and act white.

HOPE. Yeah?

DAVID. Yeah.

(They dance. Enjoying the tension.)

What sort of journalism do you do?

DAVID. Politics.

HOPE. Who do you write for?

DAVID. It's early days. I sell wherever I can. But I'm making contacts. Getting a bit of a name.

HOPE. I work for a journalist.

DAVID. You write?

HOPE. I want to. Right now I'm her assistant, and I look after her son. Along with mine.

DAVID. You've got a kid?

HOPE. Georges is two and a half. Does that surprise you?

DAVID. You married?

HOPE. No.

(The flicker of attraction grows stronger.)

So. What do you write about?

*(**DAVID** draws her closer.)*

DAVID. Things some people would rather no one wrote.

HOPE. Like what?

DAVID. Kanyaka

HOPE. What's Kanyaka?

DAVID. Corruption. Everything here is Mbongo. Grass roots to glass towers!

HOPE. *(She pronounces it wrong.)* Mbongo?

DAVID. *(He corrects her.)* Mbongo.

HOPE. Mbongo.

> *(They're flirting. Close. Turned on.* **DAVID** *speaks in a half whisper – it's exciting, clandestine, dangerous.)*

DAVID. Money and bribes. The whole mining industry here is an economic war. Tech giants, business and government, the military, all doing secret deals.

> *(***DAVID*** *lowers his voice further –)*

That's what I'm trying to unpack, trying to write about. I've got a lead on a possible big story. International corruption. Money laundering.

HOPE. *(Teasing, flirting.)* Big Billionaire Mbongo.

DAVID. It's not funny. Corruption is the norm here. It's the way it functions. Even a close friend can be bribed and turned against you. Only person you can trust is yourself.

HOPE. Do you trust yourself?

DAVID. Yes.

HOPE. Can I trust you?

> *(They are about to kiss.* **HOPE** *suddenly turns out to us.)*

The sun was setting – spilling blood red over the horizon – and when David came in me – I came too. It was so good. Better than anything before. Like suddenly I knew what all the fuss was about. I took that

sunset right into me – we melted and welded together
in a blaze of molten crimson and gold.

Scene Six – Cafe – Central London – A Few Years Later –

(A cafe. Tables.)

*(**JOHN** comes in. Sits at one. Waits. Expectant.)*

*(**ALICE** comes through the door. She stops when she sees **JOHN**.)*

(He stands. Neither of them moves for a moment. They take each other in. It's been a while.)

(They hug. They hold. A comforting.)

*(**ALICE** pulls back first. Pulls up a chair. Sits.)*

ALICE. It's good to see you.

I'm sorry I haven't been in touch.

JOHN. Thank you. For agreeing to meet.

(Awkward pause.)

ALICE. No. I wanted to. I've been meaning to –

JOHN. I wrote – when the press were decimating you –

ALICE. I know. Thank you. I appreciated it. I just – I needed to handle it alone. I'm sorry.

JOHN. You don't have to apologise – or explain –

*(The waitress comes over. [The actress who plays **HOPE**].)*

HOPE. Can I take your order?

*(**ALICE** stares at her – as if she's seen a ghost.)*

Is everything OK?

ALICE. Yes. You just remind me of – someone –

HOPE. Hope it's someone nice –

ALICE. Hope?

HOPE. Hope?

JOHN. *(Helping out.)* A latte and – an americano please – Still black no sugar?

> (**ALICE** *nods.*)

> (**HOPE** *heads off.*)

Are you OK?

ALICE. Yes. Sorry.

> (**HOPE** *carries over the coffees. She serves* **ALICE** *and* **JOHN**. *Occasionally during the scene she will hover, listening in.*)

JOHN. How is Louis?

ALICE. He's starting school this year. He's good. Full of energy. Hard work. Lovely.

> (**JOHN** *waits for her to continue. She doesn't. It's stilted between them.*)

How are your kids?

JOHN. Good. Grown up. Very. Tara's getting married. Nicolas is doing a law conversion. The twins are at Bristol.

ALICE. How's Emily?

JOHN. The same.

ALICE. The same?

> *(Beat.)*

John. Nothing is the same for me. Everything has changed.

JOHN. Have you met someone.

ALICE. No.

JOHN. OK? Thats good.

ALICE. I'm alone. But I'm not lonely. I have Louis. I'm not looking for –

>   (**ALICE** *struggles* –)

JOHN. Once the twins have left uni – once we're proper empty nesters –

ALICE. No. Don't leave her. Not for me. I don't want to be with you John.

>   (*It's awkward.* **JOHN** *struggles. The past and pain rise up in* **ALICE**.)

I fucked up didn't I. Major big time.

I'm just the latest in the long list of European Oppressors. A word hunter, a story hunter.

Hope is dead. I am alive. And it's my fault.

Nothing – Nothing I can do. I can never change that.

>   (**JOHN** *reaches for* **ALICE**'s *hand. She lets him hold it for a moment then draws her hand away.*)

JOHN. Are you working?

ALICE. No.

JOHN. Maybe you should get back into the saddle.

ALICE. No. I don't want to travel. I want to be around for Louis.

Are you working?

JOHN. You'd think at my age, my experience it would be plain sailing. But it's all change out there.

    (Beat.)

ALICE. I'm writing.

JOHN. Good. Don't want to let all that talent go to waste.

    *(**ALICE** takes a little package out of of her bag – holds it out to **JOHN**. An echo of the earlier present scene between the earlier **ALICE SEELEY HARRIS** and **JOHN HARRIS**.)*

    *(**JOHN** unwraps it. It's a manuscript. It has a title page with a picture of **ALICE SEELEY HARRIS** on it.)*

ALICE. It wasn't the book I set out to write.

It was going to be about John Harris. The missionary in the Congo who I thought was the author behind the photographs of the Atrocities in King Leopold's time. But it turned out, when I started researching – it wasn't him who took the photos. It was his wife!

JOHN. And he took the credit? What a Dastardly patriarchal privileged male.

ALICE. Those were different times.

He was knighted for it. But She didn't want to be credited. She wasn't looking for any reward other than freedom and justice it seems.

JOHN. She sounds horribly perfect.

ALICE. She wasn't. She was very conflicted. But very committed.

She rejected any attempt to foreground her. Her last wish was not to have 'Lady' written on her grave.

A quiet rebellion.

She also insisted on keeping her maiden name – 'Seeley' – against the conventions of the time. She had some hidden strength and sense of self.

(**JOHN** *flicks through the pages.*)

She had her own tragedies. As a missionary wife she had to leave her children behind in England. Her daughter Katherine later took her own life.

JOHN. Congratulations. It looks like a great read. Well done.

(*He holds it back out to* **ALICE**.)

ALICE. Keep it. That one's for you.

JOHN. Thank you.

(**JOHN** *takes the manuscript –*)

I'm staying at the Lincoln tonight. Fancy a drink at the bar later.

ALICE. I'm alright.

(*An awkward beat.*)

(**HOPE** *as a waitress comes on as they head out. She doesn't clear the table. She sweeps the cups and saucers up in the tablecloth – SWIPING it all off the table. Sort of triumphant.*)

HOPE. Now I'm dead, I've finally got my ambition back. I know what I want to be. I know what I want to do. I want to be a Doctor. A psychic surgeon. I want to reattach shards of body sensations to memories. I want to stitch the past into the present and heal pain. I want to stitch the stories back into the land. Because a country, a nation, a people, a land, is a body with memories too. Memories carried in the scars of it's mines and wars. Memories drowned in the Well of Attenuation. Memories abandoned by the Tree of Forgetfulness. I want to found a new school of medicine that sews the silenced back into our consciousness.

Scene Seven – School Playground. Seven Years Later –

> (*Cheers and cries – sounds of kids playing football. The stage is to the side of the pitch catching the edge of the floodlights.*)

> (**KASAMBAYI** *stands wrapped against the cold, hat gloves, scarf –*)

> (**ALICE** *comes out to watch the same match. She's less well dressed than* **KASAMBAYI**. *Isn't wearing gloves and has a thin coat – she sees* **KASAMBAYI** *and comes to stand near her – but just too far to be 'friends'. She shivers.*)

ALICE. Getting really cold now. I didn't dress properly for it.

> (**KASAMBAYI** *doesn't acknowledge her presence.*)

> (*The two women stare out – apart – the football shouts and cries echo and float up into the night.*)

> (**ALICE** *looks to* **KASAMBAYI**. **KASAMBAYI** *meets her eye – turns away again –*)

KASAMBAYI. Allez Georges. Go Georges! Yes yes yes YES!!!!

> (*A roar goes up from the players.* **GEORGES** *has scored.* **KASAMBAYI** *is beaming.*)

ALICE. Well done him. He's really good isn't he?

> (**KASAMBAYI** *doesn't answer.*)

It's nice the boys are going to be at secondary together.

> (**KASAMBAYI** *doesn't answer.*)

Louis talks a lot about Georges.

*(**KASAMBAYI** doesn't answer.)*

Would he like to come and play after school one day?

*(**KASAMBAYI** doesn't answer.)*

Or maybe I could drop him back to you one week after football if it helps. Would save us both waiting –

KASAMBAYI. I like to watch him play.

*(Another long beat. **ALICE** dares.)*

ALICE. Mrs Mabele. I know nothing I can ever say or do is going to make up for your loss. I regret what happened every day. I regret what I did.

KASAMBAYI. It's not just my loss. Georges lost his mother.

(They both concentrate on the game again.)

*(**KASAMBAYI**'s phone goes. She answers.)*

KASAMBAYI. Demain soir c'est pas possible. I can do in the day. Not evenings. I have my grandson. Alright. Oui oui. Je vais essayer. OK.

*(**KASAMBAYI** hangs up. She looks to **ALICE**. She hesitates – then.)*

Georges would like to play with Louis after school tomorrow.

ALICE. Yes. I could do that.

KASAMBAYI. How much?

ALICE. Nothing. It would be a play date. We'd love it.

KASAMBAYI. I need childcare. I'm part of an organisation against violence to women in the Congo. We meet twice a week in evenings. I can't take Georges. It's not a place for him.

ALICE.   Of course not. I'm happy to help. It sounds amazing. What do you do?

KASAMBAYI.   We raise awareness. We fund raise. We send money out to Congo to Bisie for a woman's refuge.

ALICE.   An extra child is no problem. Whenever you need. Really.

       (**KASAMBAYI** *turns back to the pitch.*)

       (*They watch the game.*)

KASAMBAYI.   Allez. Go Louis. Good save. He's coming on.

       (*The two women stand side by side. Silent. Looking out at the pitch.*)

       (*Hope comes between the two women. she takes* **ALICE***'s hand in one of her hands and her mother's hand in the other. She forms the ghostly link that somehow bonds and binds them.*)

Scene Eight – A Lecture Hall. London Present and London 1904 –

(An assistant comes in and sets up a modern state-of-the-art screen with a mic; power point screen, and a computer on an electronically controlled screen.)

(The **CHAIR** *comes in and takes the mic –)*

CHAIR. It is with immense pleasure that I would like to introduce you to our next speaker. She is the founder of the charity 'Hope', a transformational leadership community for women survivors of violence, located in the Eastern Democratic Republic of Congo. The charity aims to heal women from their past trauma through therapy and life skills programming while providing them with the essential ingredients needed to move forward in life – love and community. Please welcome to the stage – Kasambayi Mabele.

*(**KASAMBAYI** comes in. She has a pile of papers that she is reading through and a pencil to make last minute amendments. She's dressed smartly.)*

*(**KASAMBAYI** steps up to the podium. She taps the mic. Yes it's working.)*

KASAMBAYI. Hello everyone. I am honoured to be asked to speak here tonight. My name is Kasambayi Mabele. I come from a small mining village in the East Congo – a little town which no longer exists. It was burned to the ground. The women were raped and their wombs colonised by the soldiers. Or they were shot. The older male children and men were taken to work in the mines. The older female children were taken as wives for the soldiers. The very old and very young were killed. Very few of us survived. I was fortunate enough to be one of those that did.

I am here to tell you my story. Just one small story among thousands – for many years I didn't tell my story. Rape survivors are not welcome. We are shame for husbands, parents and communities. I never told my daughter the true story of her beginning. I wanted to save her from shame. I would do it differently if I had the chance again. I would tell her how proud I was to have brought her into the world. I wish I had told her the truth because then she wouldn't have had to go hunting for it herself.

I used to work in the fields in a small village in Walungu territory. My husband worked in the mines. We had two little son's Monoka and Makeise. Monoka means rain because he was born in the rains. Makeise means Joy because he made us laugh with the expression he came out wearing.

One night I heard a knock on the door. Outside were men in army uniforms. I hid under the bed with the children and the little money we had. My husband opened the door to them. They wanted food and money. They took all they found, our radio too. Then Monoka woke. I couldn't hush him. He started crying. They pulled us out from under the bed. They took the money. They told my husband they would punish him for lying. They shot my children. They made my husband watch while they raped me. Then they shot him. They cut my hand off but they didn't kill me.

The main weapon of this conflict isn't guns, or grenades or machetes, though those weapons help to keep fear alive. The main weapon of the war is systematic rape. It is cheaper than bullets and it guarantees that you are destroying the community.

When a woman is raped she is kicked out of her village – we women perform practical duties, we raise the children, we till the fields, emotionally and spiritually we hold the family together. Throwing the women out wrenches the heart out of the community. Rips up the village by its roots.

Today in Congo, human exploitation and degradation and forced labour and child labour are not a thing of the past – every gigabyte of memory on your device, every rechargeable battery you use, is paid for in blood.

> (**KASAMBAYI** *takes out her phone and places it on the table before her.*)

> (**HOPE** *steps forward. There's something of Kae Tempest about her. Something spoken word.*)

> (*She moves freely around the stage. Fluid. Powerful. Full of energy. Dionysian. Not victim like at all. Celebratory.*)

HOPE. My mother hid her pain. Buried her secret in her body. But it bred.

Gave birth to me and somewhere there passed on the story too. Stories are like seeds. They wait until it's time to germinate. They have a patience. They have a life force.

I remembered anyway.

Scene Nine – Kasambayi's Kitchen – Some Years in The Future –

(**KASAMBAYI** *sings loudly along to her iPhone which blares out Congolese gospel music. She sings at the top her her voice along with the congregation, stopping occasionally to make sure she's in time with them...*)

(*She wears the same brightly coloured African cloth wrapped around her waist that she did at the start of the play, and a simple T-shirt. She has a huge plastic bucket in front of her on the floor and is bent over it. As she sings she makes beignet. Mixing together flour and water and sugar to make small round doughnut balls ready to deep fat fry. She exudes fierce goodwill.*)

(**HOPE** *come in and jumps up onto the sideboard, but* **KASAMBAYI** *doesn't see her.*)

HOPE. If a mother gave birth to a child.

She can still be reborn by the child.

(*A young man comes in. It's* **GEORGES**, *he's twenty two. He's got his own headphones in and he is swaying and moving to the beat.*)

KASAMBAYI. Georges! Georges!

(*But* **GEORGES** *doesn't hear.* **KASAMBAYI** *looks to him full of love.*)

HOPE. Memory lives in the fibres of the soul. In the muscles. In the instinct. Smuggled in the blood. Learned by the lungs, held by the heart – burnt in the brain. It's a whisper and a warning from the past.

It's where your ancestors roots meet the first flush of life in you.

>   (**GEORGES** *is still dancing.*)

KASAMBAYI. Georges! Georges!

>   (**GEORGES** *doesn't clock her, she throws a cloth at him playfully – and he jerks out of his world. He pulls his headphones out. She switches off her phone.*)

Have you heard?

>   (**GEORGES** *suddenly stands very still, nods his head giving nothing away.*)

And?

>   (**GEORGES** *sighs, shakes his head, lowers it.*)

But you worked so hard.

>   (**GEORGES** *looks sad, then suddenly he can't keep the secret any longer it bubbles up into laughter.*)

GEORGES. I did it! I got in!

>   (**KASAMBAYI** *bursts into tears and laughter.*)

>   (**HOPE** *on the sideboard claps her hands and cheers.*)

KASAMBAYI. *Oh Georges. Oh Georges.*

>   (**GEORGES** *runs to his granny and envelops her in a huge hug. She hugs him and he hugs her. He gets her to dance round the kitchen with him.*)

I am so proud of you. I am SO proud!

*(**HOPE** moves into the centre of the stage for her epilogue.)*

HOPE. In the hope of green shoots and fresh water.

Our spirits will grow again

Will wave in the wind and unfurl,

Our stories will take seed again,

We will not be buried.

We will re-root.

The End

Ingram Content Group UK Ltd.
Milton Keynes UK
UKHW021953120623
423315UK00014B/996